Captain Cook *was here*

Over eight days and eight nights in late April of 1770, Captain Cook and the men of the *Endeavour* made their first extended landfall on the east coast of New Holland. The ensuing events and interactions between the voyagers and the indigenous inhabitants were marked by drama and intrigue, courage and fear.

But the story does not end with the *Endeavour* sailing away. The original encounter on land between the British mariners and the first Australians has been one of Australia's founding legends. Bringing together first-hand historical accounts, oral narratives, surviving objects and artefacts plus much of the artwork produced during Cook's time on shore, Maria Nugent takes a challenging new look at the impact of Cook's arrival on the land and on its people.

Captain Cook Was Here reconnects with the stories that all Australians – Aboriginal and non-Aboriginal – have told through their art, history and folklore.

Maria Nugent is Research Fellow in the Centre for Historical Research at the National Museum of Australia and in the School of Historical Studies at Monash University. She is the author of *Botany Bay: Where Histories Meet*, which won the New South Wales Premier's Community and Regional History Prize in 2006.

Captain Cook was here

Maria Nugent

www.cambridge.org

Shaftesbury Road, Cambridge CB2 8EA, United Kingdom

One Liberty Plaza, 20th Floor, New York, NY 10006, USA

477 Williamstown Road, Port Melbourne, VIC 3207, Australia

314–321, 3rd Floor, Plot 3, Splendor Forum, Jasola District Centre, New Delhi – 110025, India

103 Penang Road, #05–06/07, Visioncrest Commercial, Singapore 238467

Cambridge University Press is part of Cambridge University Press & Assessment, a department of the University of Cambridge.

We share the University's mission to contribute to society through the pursuit of education, learning and research at the highest international levels of excellence.

www.cambridge.org
Information on this title: www.cambridge.org/9780521762403

© Maria Nugent 2009

This publication is in copyright. Subject to statutory exception and to the provisions of relevant collective licensing agreements, no reproduction of any part may take place without the written permission of Cambridge University Press & Assessment.

First published 2009

Designed & typeset by Rob Cowpe Design

A catalogue record for this publication is available from the British Library

National Library of Australia Cataloguing in Publication data
   Nugent, Maria.
   Captain Cook was here / Maria Nugent.
   9780521762403 (hbk.)
   Includes index.
   Bibliography
   Cook, James, 1728–1779.
   Botany Bay (N.S.W.)—History.
   Botany Bay (N.S.W.)—Discovery and exploration.
994.4101

ISBN   978-0-521-76240-3   Hardback

Reproduction and communication for educational purposes
The Australian Copyright Act 1968 (the Act) allows a maximum of one chapter or 10% of the pages of this publication, whichever is the greater, to be reproduced and/or communicated by any educational institution for its educational purposes provided that the educational institution (or the body that administers it) has given a remuneration notice to Copyright Agency Limited (CAL) under the Act.

For details of the CAL licence for educational institutions contact:

Copyright Agency Limited
Level 15, 233 Castlereagh Street
Sydney NSW 2000
Telephone: (02) 9394 7600
Facsimile: (02) 9394 7601
Email: info@copyright.com.au

Reproduction and communication for other purposes
Except as permitted under the Act (for example a fair dealing for the purposes of study, research, criticism or review) no part of this publication may be reproduced, stored in a retrieval system, communicated or transmitted in any form or by any means without prior written permission. All inquiries should be made to the publisher at the address above.

Cambridge University Press & Assessment has no responsibility for the persistence or accuracy of URLs for external or third-party internet websites referred to in this publication, and does not guarantee that any content on such websites is, or will remain, accurate or appropriate. Information regarding prices, travel timetables, and other factual information given in this work is correct at the time of first printing but Cambridge University Press & Assessment does not guarantee the accuracy of such information thereafter.

Indigenous readers are respectfully advised that some people mentioned in writing or depicted in photographs in the following pages have passed away.

Contents

Prologue	VII
In the beginning	**1**
The first day	3
Always beginning	23
The first day continued	39
In between	**49**
The second day	51
The third day	62
The fourth day	69
The fifth day	82
The sixth day	85
The seventh day	92
In the end	**97**
The eighth day	99
Never ending	105
The Endeavour sails	137
Sources	138
List of illustrations	149
Acknowledgments	151
Index	153

Prologue

Captain Cook was here. That's common knowledge among many, if not most, Australians. But what did he do while he was here? Charted and named the eastern coastline, certainly. Explored and described parts of the country, definitely. Got his ship stuck on the coral, famously. Claimed the entire east coast for his King in England, controversially. But is that all?

Much of this book is taken up with a detailed account of the days that Cook and company spent at and around the place he eventually called Botany Bay, which is situated a short distance south of the present-day metropolis of Sydney. This was the expedition's very first landfall on the east coast of the Australian continent. The men on the *Endeavour* came ashore at this place with expectations as yet untested by experience. Here they encountered up close for the first time the country and its people, both of which they had been observing at a distance across water for over a week as the *Endeavour* sailed northwards after falling in with the coastline at the place that Cook called Point Hicks.

Their stay at this bay lasted eight days and eight nights. It began early one Saturday morning in the last week of April 1770 and ended early on a Sunday morning at the start of May. One week and one day. It's time enough to get acquainted with a place and the people who live there.

Cook's acquaintance with the local people, his and his companions' interactions with them, and their various awkward attempts 'to form a connection with the natives' as Cook describes it in his journal, is the main thread in the eight-day story that I present in these pages. Interacting with and trying to interact with the local people in this place occupies a fair portion of the voyagers' written accounts, particularly those penned by Cook himself but also those by others who accompanied him, Joseph Banks included. The topic shares the pages of their journals with details about the changeability of the weather, the everyday employments of the crew, the varying size of the daily hauls of fish, and the singularities of the country.

Yet despite the voyagers' obvious interest in the locals and the effort they expended in seeking to meet with them, the theme has been largely downplayed in Australian histories of Captain Cook. Cook's interactions with the locals have been, by and large, of only passing or secondary interest. Australian historians and writers have generally preferred to concentrate on Cook's voyaging, or his map-making, or the imperial context within which he lived. Or they have focused instead on the botany that Joseph Banks collected during this landfall, turning his flower-hunting into the most important thing to have happened upon this shore. The voyagers' interactions and relations with the locals have often been little more than a footnote, mentioned but dismissed as unimportant or non-existent or, if examined at all, largely misconstrued.

This inattention is a peculiarly Australian phenomenon, not evident in the historical and other scholarship produced in other places that Cook visited on his voyages, such as New Zealand and Hawai'i. Some would argue that this is because the encounters on the Australian east coast were by comparison few and not as sustained or as close as they were in other parts of the Pacific, but that's really no reason to give them short shrift.

The one encounter that most people in Australia have at least an inkling about is the strained standoff on the beach at Botany Bay, when Cook and his men attempted to make their first landing and some local men came down to the shore to warn or ward them off. The story is often told, because for much of the twentieth century – and still in some quarters – it's considered one of the nation's foundational moments, but despite this, or because of it, the incident itself is little understood. Mythologising has obscured other interpretations of it, and blocked from view all the other interactions that took place over the days and nights that followed.

PROLOGUE

And so a common misconception about Cook's first stopover on the east coast is that there was no interaction with the locals, or at least none to really speak of. But this is not so. Cook's own words and those of his companions give the lie to that. The accounts that James Cook, Joseph Banks, Sydney Parkinson, Zachary Hicks and others on the Endeavour give in their journals about dealings with the local people are full of surprises. Their descriptions evoke the drama, fragility, humanity, intrigue and regret of the situation. Sometimes these chroniclers provide only a cryptic comment, so condensed that it takes effort and imagination to pick away at its possible meanings. On other occasions they are more expansive, giving one detail and then another and perhaps one more, so that something of the dynamism of the experienced or witnessed incident is conveyed. Whether brief or fulsome, they all point to the sustained presence of the local people while the voyagers were in their country, and their enduring efforts to deal with these strangers from the sea.

One way to try to make sense of what the local people were doing in response to the voyagers is to sequence their actions as they are described in the various voyage journals and logs. And so, in the pages that follow is a day-by-day, episode-by-episode account of those eight days and eight nights. By tracking their interactions sequentially, showing how one incident has the capacity to trigger another or to escalate a situation for better or worse, and by treating them as actual lived experiences involving individuals situated in a particular time and place, the story of Captain Cook in Australia comes into view in a new way. This approach draws attention to the local people's creative and conscious efforts to deal in tolerable ways with this strange situation – and it presents Captain Cook in new garb. He appears in this narrative not simply as the accomplished navigator, or the one-dimensional imperial hero, but also as possessing in embryonic form an ethnographer's bent.

The local people had little choice but to confront, and engage and tolerate as best they could, the presence over days and nights of this shipload of strange men in their country and in their midst. Captain Cook was here in *their* place, the place that they called home, or whatever comparable concept they had that might be glossed today as home. Captain Cook was here *in their country, in their waters, in their domicile, in their midst, in their presence*. The location of this history is theirs.

Yet the catchcry 'Captain Cook was here' has underwritten a very different history from this local indigenous one. It's a claim that has been chorused and celebrated by generations of Australians after British

PROLOGUE

colonisation in 1788. The fact that once upon a time Captain Cook was here was sometimes used in imaginative ways to tie this antipodean place to the imperial centre. *Captain Cook was here* became a shorthand way of saying that the territory belonged to the British. *Captain Cook was here* is an opening line in histories of the Australian nation.

And so the story about what Cook did when he was actually here cannot be easily disentangled or simply stand separate from the story about the ways in which his presence in this place, his days on these shores and his descriptions of what he saw have been interpreted by historians and other storytellers and incorporated into the histories that settler Australians have since told themselves about their place in this place. Through images, through performances, through texts and through symbols, a story about settler Australians making their own meaning from the material of Captain Cook's past actions can also be found in the pages that follow.

Likewise, the story about the ways in which settler Australians have made history from Captain Cook's activities on and along the east coast cannot be easily disentangled or simply stand separate from the story about the ways in which Aboriginal Australians have also spent two centuries or more making sense about what happened when Captain Cook was here, and unmaking (or unmasking) the stories that settler Australians have told about that time. Through their storytelling, in spoken word and visual image especially, Aboriginal people across the continent, in places where Cook went and in others where he did not go, offer their own original interpretations about the encounter between the local people and Captain Cook and his men. The fact that once upon a time Captain Cook was here is a means for talking about and explaining complex and fraught histories concerning relations between Aboriginal people and 'the white people'. In their reworkings of recognisable images of Captain Cook, Aboriginal people question the plot of Australian history that begins with him, and remind their audiences about their prior and continuing claims to and presence in this place.

When it comes to the matter of Captain Cook in Australia as well as in Australian history and imagination, one might say that it's a classic case of *always beginning, never ending*. This is a story still in the process of being told, a history that is constantly in the making. There is always something new, or more, to say. There is no last word, or at least none yet said. By plaiting a narrative about the interactions between the local people and the *Endeavour*'s men that took place over a week and one day in 1770 with stories about Captain Cook told by Aboriginal and non-Aboriginal Australians over two centuries or more, my intention is to show something of that open-ended quality, to reflect upon the lively and constant interplay between past and present, and to propose yet more possibilities for interpreting this particular past and its many and changing meanings.

Captain Cook was here.
    Always beginning.
        Never ending.

In the BEGINNING

The FIRST DAY

'At day light in the morning we discovered a bay', recorded James Cook in his journal under the date of 28 April 1770. A discovery – the finding of something new – at dawn, the start of a new day. It was a good beginning.

'An opening appearing like a harbour was seen and we stood directly in for it' is how Joseph Banks recorded the event in his journal. The opening to the bay is difficult to miss when sailing up the coast, because its northern headland pokes out beyond the southern coastline like an overbite. As Cook noted in a short section providing future sailors with directions for locating this safe anchorage,

> in coming from the Southward it is discoverd before you are abreast of it which you cannot do in coming from the northward; the entrance is little more than a Mile broad and lies in WNW.

From Cook's point of view, the bay looked promising because it 'appeard to be tolerably well shelterd from all winds'. An attempt to land the previous day on the open coast a short distance to the south had been prevented by 'reason of the great surf which beat every where upon the shore'. And so a sheltered bay without breakers was a welcome sight for a ship's captain keen to land. Four weeks had passed since leaving the west coast of New Zealand at the place that Cook called Cape Farewell. It was time to stop. 'Voyagers would stop', the historian Greg Dening reminds us, 'to refurbish their ships or they came to trade or they came because they needed a stopping place on their way to somewhere else'. The somewhere else in this instance was home. Cook's first voyage to the South Seas was on its last leg. However, there was still much work to do and many miles to cover. Some of the sailors who were participants in and witnesses to what would happen at this particular stopping place over the days that followed did not survive the journey back to England.

Cook's decision to sail westwards from the west coast of New Zealand with the intention of meeting with the east coast of New Holland had been one of three alternatives. One option was to sail to the east in the direction of Cape Horn with the hope of determining once and for all the existence or otherwise of the great southern land. This was the most desired course because of its potential for great discoveries. But it would be a long way around for a ship that had already been at sea for nearly two years. It was too risky and so was not pursued. A second option was to sail to the south of Van Diemen's Land and directly to the Cape of Good Hope. This route would be short on discoveries, but it would be a quick and certain way home. This was the least desirable plan, and so was passed over in favour of the third option. This was to sail to the west. As Cook explained in his journal,

> until we fell in with the East Coast of New Holland and then to steer the direction of that coast to the northward or what other direction it may take until we arrive at its northern extremity, and if this should be found impractical then to endeavour to fall in with the lands or islands discovered by Quiros [in 1606].

No grand discovery would be made along this route, but there would be some interest along the way that would provide a modest compensation for not having located the elusive southern continent. Banks wrote,

> In doing this, although we hoped to make discoveries more interesting to trade at least than any we had yet made, we were obliged intirely to give up our first grand object, the Southern Continent: this for my own part I confess I could not do without much regret.

As the Endeavour loitered at the entrance to this bay on New Holland's east coast, Banks did not yet know it but this would be the place for some of his most interesting and most famous botanical discoveries. They would be, one suspects, a salve for his initial regret.

THE FIRST DAY

And so 'into [the bay] I resolved to go with the Ship', Cook wrote, 'and with this view sent the Master in the Pinnace to sound the entrance while we kept turning up the Ship having the wind right out'. Nigel Erskine, a curator at the Australian National Maritime Museum in Sydney, has kindly translated Cook's maritime vernacular. Commenting on this passage, he says:

> *It seems Cook was keeping the Endeavour from making any headway which would take him away from the entrance to Botany Bay until the pinnace returned. I interpret 'we kept turning up' to mean turning the vessel up into the wind. In this manoeuvre, the ship moves as if it is going to tack through the eye of the wind but fails to do so and is effectively 'in irons' with all the sails aback – or 'having the wind right out' of them. It is a way of stopping the ship in the water.*

Robert Molyneux was the master sent in the pinnace to sound the entrance to the bay at nine in the morning. He was twenty-two years of age and already a veteran of voyaging to the South Seas. As master's mate, he had sailed with Captain Samuel Wallis on the *Dolphin* between 1766 and 1768 – the expedition that became famous for 'discovering' Tahiti. So this was not his first expedition; but it would be his last. He died just out of Cape Town as the *Endeavour* was embarking on the home stretch. However, that was still almost a year away. He kept a log for part of the voyage, which includes tantalising descriptions of the ship's time in Tahiti, but it ends in October 1769. He also kept a journal, which continued for a few months longer but its last entry was 9 January 1770, before the *Endeavour* reached this bay, so we do not have any testimony from him about the east coast of New Holland.

In the log, he condenses a full day into a few lines, listing all the major occurrences but elaborating none of them. I wonder if his verbal reports to his captain, or his conversational mode, were the same. A portrait of him in New Zealand's Hocken Library shows a fine-featured face with a long nose, a high forehead and a confident gaze (Plate 2). Upon Molyneux' death, Cook commented in his journal that he was a 'young man of good parts, but had unfortunately given himself up to extravagancy and intemperance which brought on disorders that put period to his life'. In the portrait there's little sign of the penchant for extravagance that Cook claimed killed him.

From on board the ship, Banks saw through glasses about ten people gathered around a fire on the north head 'at a very barren place'. Soon afterwards, the group 'retir'd to a little eminence where they could conveniently see the ship', said Banks. He observed closely every move of the people he saw on the shore. He noted for instance that four more men came to join those who were already gathered on the headland. Those four men had arrived in two canoes, which they pulled up onto a beach immediately below the cliff. Who knows from where they had come, or what they had been doing prior to joining the others. Fishing in the shallows further inside the bay, perhaps. Spying on the ship, possibly. At this point, the pinnace approached the north point where this group had gathered. As it did so, the people 'all retird higher up on the hill', except one who hid behind some rocks where he remained the entire time. He was a man on lookout duty.

'Sounding' is an apt word for what the men in the pinnace were doing on this day. They tested not only the depth of the water but also incidentally the feelings of the local people. As the pinnace was rowed around the coves close to the shore with the men on board regularly dropping and drawing the lead, some local men followed it. They initially followed at a distance. But then, within a cove, 'a little within the harbour', they came down to the beach and, according to Banks, they

> invited our people to land by many signs and word[s] which he did not understand; all however were armd with long pikes and a wooden weapon made something like a short scymetar.

Banks had got this report verbally from Molyneux when he returned to the ship.

'Invited our people to land by signs and word[s] which they could not understand'. This is one of those phrases penned by mariners in unfamiliar places that encapsulate the essence of the experience of cross-cultural encounter. There is a statement of understanding followed by an admission of non-understanding. The sentence has its own internal contradiction. It captures the tension inherent in trying to make sense of things in the absence of a shared language and in situations with little or no precedence. Could the men in the pinnace be certain that the signs the local people made were an invitation to them to land? Are gestures of invitation universal? If they could not understand the words spoken, then how did they know they were not in fact being told to go away?

Sentences like this are worth noticing because they serve as reminders of the uncertainties that characterise all cross-cultural encounters. It can be tempting to read the words of men like James Cook and Joseph Banks as though they provide clear windows onto past events. Yet it is surely mistaken to take Cook or Banks or any other of the journal writers on board the *Endeavour* completely at their word. The issue is not that they are unreliable witnesses or liars or fabricators. The problem is not even to do with the limits of language to represent something called reality. Rather, the crux of the matter lies in the very nature of the experience of meeting strangers, of encountering others, of having one's communications lost in translation. The mariners who wrote journals, particularly detailed and lengthy journals such as those produced by Banks and Cook, were themselves grasping for the right words to represent their experiences of encounters with people whose language, spoken and gestural, they did not comprehend. Not surprising then that they sometimes found themselves lost for words, or made contradictory statements, or crossed out what they had written, or later inserted something new over old text. Their writing is a testament to their struggle to make sense. As they wrote down what they saw and what happened, the mariners guessed at the meanings of things with varying degrees of certainty.

Like the men sounding the entrance, we cannot be sure what the local people were trying to convey with their signs and sounds. Unlike them, we have the advantage of being able to draw on later sources that describe aspects of the social life of the local people who lived on this part of the coast or further afield. These other, later sources provoke ideas about ways in which it might be possible to interpret some of the descriptions provided by Cook, Banks and others. Although the material available about the local people in this part of the country is certainly not comprehensive, it can be complemented with material from other regions. However, drawing comparisons and correspondences between one group and another should be done with some caution. This was a country of not one people, but of many different groups. Probably the greatest challenge is to compare the records from Cook's own time with ethnographic and other accounts based on observations made in later periods, when the situation of local groups had changed through the conditions brought about by colonisation. Nonetheless, this mosaic of material is 'at least suggestive of the indigenous societies and cultures that existed earlier'. Suggestiveness informs speculation. It's better than nothing.

Ethnographies of indigenous groups that were produced in the nineteenth and twentieth centuries, such as A. W. Howitt's *The Native Tribes of South-East Australia* (first published in 1904) can help. In a short section on gesture language, Howitt suggests that among some groups 'a stranger . . . seen . . . from afar . . . can be interrogated at a safe distance by gesture language as to who he is, where he comes from, and his intentions'. Could this have been the meaning of the signs interpreted by the men in the sounding boat as an invitation to land?

Banks continued closely watching the local men who had remained on the headland while the others followed the sounding boat around the coves. He had watched them watching him watch them. He wrote,

> During this time a few of the Indians who had not followd the boat remaind on the rocks opposite the ship, threatening and menacing with their pikes and swords — two in particular who were painted with white, their faces seemingly only dusted over with it, their bodies painted with broad strokes drawn over their breasts and backs resembling much a soldiers cross belts, and their legs and thighs also with such like broad strokes drawn round them which imitated broad garters or bracelets.

Banks again describes the way in which each of the two men held in his hand a wooden weapon 'about 2½ feet long, in shape much resembling a scymeter'. (A 'scymeter', or scimitar, is a sword that is short and curved. A common assumption is that Banks used the comparison in an attempt to describe a boomerang, but it was more likely that the object he observed was a type of curved wooden club, sometimes known as a waddy.) And all the while they 'seemed to talk earnestly together, at times brandishing their crooked weapons at us in token of defiance'.

A 'token of defiance'. Not an invitation to fight. Not even defiance itself. A sign or show or display of defiance. Banks was aware that there was a performance in process on the point opposite the ship as it waited for the pinnace to return. He was not interpreting their behaviour simply in terms of straightforward combat, or outright aggression, which is the way that later settler Australian storytellers would commonly present it. During the long voyage so far, he had observed on more than one occasion the function that performances had when strangers arrived. But he knew, as did Cook, that 'there was always a fine line between dramatised and actual threat'. On this occasion, as it turned out, James Cook was not prepared to spend much time testing where that line might lie in this new and strange place.

Joseph Banks had a copy of William Dampier's 1699 voyage journal with him. Presuming he had read it closely, he could well have anticipated this scene. When Dampier and his men were digging for water in the sand on the north-west coast seventy years earlier there came '9 or 10 of the Natives to a small Hill a little way from us, and stood there menacing and threatening us, and making a great Noise'. 'Menacing and threatening'

— Banks had used the same words as Dampier when he sought to describe what he saw. And there would be many mariners who touched the coast of the continent after Banks and Cook who would be greeted in this way by the local people. Eighteen years later, waving weapons welcomed the leading ships of the convict-bearing convoy (now known rather grandly and capitalised as the 'First Fleet' — a title that could only be ascribed in the wake of a second fleet being sent out from Britain). As one witness described that episode in a letter home: 'The Natives as we Sail'd in came Down to the edge of the Cliffs Making a Noise & Lifting up their spears'.

One of the local men Dampier had encountered on the north-west coast in 1699 was wearing body paint. He had

> a Circle of white Paste or Pigment (a sort of Lime, as we thought) about his Eyes, and a white streak down his Nose from his Forehead to the tip of it. And his Breast and some part of his Arms were also made white with the same Paint,

wrote Dampier in his account. He surmised that this man, adorned as he was, was a leader. A hundred years after Dampier, the navigator Matthew Flinders touched on the south-west coast while circumnavigating the continent. There he noted the way in which the local people one morning had admired the marines' 'red coats and white crossed belts . . . having some resemblance to their own manner of ornamenting themselves'. This time it seems it was Banks who was being plagiarised, because he had described the pattern of the marks on the bodies of the men on the headland while the *Endeavour* lingered at the entrance to this bay as being 'like a soldier's cross belts'.

According to the archaeologist Sylvia Hallam, body decoration 'created a sense of occasion, turning an encounter into a formal meeting, and heightening everyone's awareness of the importance of the occasion'. This comes from an article by Hallam, published in 1983, about meetings or encounters between local people and various 'outsiders' on the western side of the continent. Through assembling an archive of descriptions taken from voyage journals, explorer accounts, colonial memoirs and ethnographic studies describing what happened when local groups came into contact with people who were strangers to them — whether those strangers were other indigenous people, maritime voyagers, early explorers, or new settlers — Hallam is able to provide a broad typology of the actions and reactions of the local group encountered. Some of the behaviours she describes chime with the things that Banks, especially, recorded in his journal on the day the *Endeavour* arrived in this bay, such as the weapon waving and the loud shouting and the body decoration. If one compares the occurrence in 1770 with other recorded episodes on other beaches around the vast coastline, it becomes quite clear that the local people were behaving in ways consistent with practices employed by other groups elsewhere across the continent, and at times both before and after 1770. They were acting – at the outset at least – in customary ways. This was a meeting with strangers.

In Banks' retinue was Sydney Parkinson, a draughtsman who had had to assume most of the responsibility for making illustrations of things seen on the voyage after the death in Tahiti of Alexander Buchan, another artist whom Banks had brought along. A portrait of Parkinson, believed to be a self-portrait, held in the Natural History Museum in London shows him rosy-lipped and wide-eyed (Plate 3). On a page of sketches he made while at this bay are rough drawings of two men with painted bodies (Plate 4). The models might have been these two men on the headland, bodies painted, weapons held aloft. The artist went to some trouble to illustrate their body decorations, showing the bands around the thighs and below the knees on one of them and the pattern on the chest of the other.

In making these sketches, Parkinson's purpose was to make 'personal notes, not scientific records', the art historian Bernard Smith explains. These rough drawings were *aides de memoire* from which the artist hoped to work up more detailed illustrations, although it seems that he was unable to do so before he died on the return journey to England. Later images of local men around Port Jackson made by artists in the opening years of the British settlement document similar body adornment. A picture by the enigmatic 'Port Jackson Painter', for instance, of a man known as Balloderree shows strokes of white paste underneath his eyes and drawn diagonally from each of his shoulders meeting at a point in the middle of his chest. Describing this decoration, John White, an officer in the first fleet, wrote in his journal in early 1788 that 'many of their warriors ... we observed to be painted with stripes across the breast and back, which at some little distance appears not unlike our soldiers' cross belts'. This is the same recognisable military image being used again to create a correspondence between something familiar and something unfamiliar.

After the soundings had been taken, by noon the *Endeavour* 'working to windward' sailed into the bay towards the southern shore, where an hour and a half later it came to 'with the best bower in sandy ground', as most of the ship's logs explain. The local men who had decorated their bodies, who had brandished their weapons, who had shouted at the ship, were left behind on the north headland. They presumably stood watching the ship make its way towards the southern shore of this wide bay.

In the wake of this expedition, the place that Cook eventually called Botany Bay came to be conceived as one single geographical entity. The name he ascribed to it covers the immediate hinterland of the northern and southern headlands and the western shoreline, and the expanse of water embraced by them. This is the extent of the country that Cook charted during his short stay. But it is worth bearing in mind, as we follow the Endeavour's men around the landscape during the eight days they spent here, and particularly as they criss-crossed from the north shore to the south shore and back again, that they were probably passing out of the territory of one group of local people and into the territory of another. They were doing something that the local people themselves might not have often done, or not as freely as these strangers did.

The local people who lived on the southern shore of the bay referred to themselves as the Gweagal, although Cook and his men were not able to ascertain this detail while they were there. Despite what some contemporary historians say, there is little solid evidence that a list of words was collected by the mariners from the local people during this particular encounter. There was not the opportunity to exchange very much at all, let alone words. The identification of these people as Gweagal emerges from later encounters in and around this place. David Collins, judge-advocate in the government of the British settlement at Sydney in 1788, investigated and recorded the names that various groups of local people called themselves. While explaining a point about social organisation, he wrote in a book he published that:

> Each family has a particular place of residence, from which is derived its distinguishing name: thus the southern shore of Botany Bay is called Gwea, and the people who inhabit it stile [sic] themselves Gweagal.

The people on the western shore of the bay, north of what later became known as the Georges River, were the Gameygal, that is, the people from Gamey (also spelt Gamay or Kamay). The name that the people on the north side of the bay used for themselves is less certain. These days they sometimes appear as the Bediagal on maps that attempt to represent the Sydney landscape as it was before colonisation, but that's more than likely inaccurate.

The expanse of water in the wide bay and the two rivers on its western shore were natural borders between neighbouring groups. While it is impossible to reconstruct precisely the distribution of all the clans, it is quite clear that in the late eighteenth-century period, when Cook stopped by briefly and when the convicts and their overseers came to stay, the people on the north side of the bay spoke a language different from that of the people on the south, who were speakers of the Dharawal language. According to the archaeologist Peter Turbet, the Gweagal were the northernmost speakers of that language. Groups on the north of the bay spoke what some linguists refer to as the Sydney language.

It's likely that language was not the only difference between these groups. Early colonial accounts suggest some enmity between those who lived north of this wide bay and those who lived on its southern side, and at times ascribe to them different temperaments. Rumour around the first British settlement at Sydney Cove was that the people on the southern side of Botany Bay were a fierce mob. The navigator and explorer Matthew Flinders claimed that they had a reputation among the local people around Port Jackson for being 'exceedingly ferocious, if not cannibals'. While this slur was certainly overblown, it is suggestive of the ways in which the local people living in and around the Sydney settlement in the closing years of the eighteenth century considered their neighbours, or at least characterised them to the colonists living in their midst.

As the *Endeavour* crossed the water towards its eventual anchorage point under the southern shore, it shared the surface of the sheltered bay with four small canoes. Banks describes the scene.

> ... [in] each of these was one man who held in his hand a long pole with which he struck fish, venturing with his little imbarkation almost into the surf. These people seemd to be totally engag'd in what they were about: the ship passd within a quarter of a mile of them and yet they scarce lifted their eyes from their employment; I was almost inclined to think that attentive to their business and deafned by the noise of the surf they neither saw nor heard her go past them.

It is possible that the men fishing did not hear or see the ship go past, as Banks was inclined to believe, or they may have had no choice even in the presence of a strange ship but to fish when the fish were running. Perhaps they had decided on a course of action for dealing with these seaborne strangers, which involved keeping their distance. Or maybe this was a performance too, part of the local people's usual response to strangers in their midst, a strategy that complemented their efforts to engage with the strangers in a more vociferous way. The practice of ignoring strangers, as Hallam explains, was one element within a repeating pattern sometimes used in dealings with strangers. Other elements in the sequence were avoiding strangers and repelling them. Before too long, these other two dispositions would be displayed by the local people on the south shore towards the mariners.

The Endeavour was brought to anchor at about half-past one in the afternoon and the boats were hoisted out soon afterwards, according to the ship's logs. However, the landing party did not prepare to row ashore until about three o'clock. In the hour-and-a-half interim, the sailors sat down to their midday meal. The people on the shore were seen to do the same. Describing the anchorage point near the south shore, Cook mentioned that there were a 'few hutts, Men, women and children abreast of the Ship'. Banks describes the ship as at anchor 'abreast of a small village consisting of about 6 or 8 houses'. The ship had pulled up close to where some local people lived.

Banks narrates with some sympathy the sequence of actions he observed in the small village on the shore.

> *An old woman followd by three children came out of the wood; she carried several piece[s] of stick and the children also had their little burthens; when she came to the houses 3 more younger children came out of one of them to meet her. She often lookd at the ship but expressd neither surprise nor concern. Soon after this she lighted a fire and the four Canoes came in from fishing; the people landed, hauld up their boats and began to dress their dinner to all appearance totally unmoved at us, tho we were within a little more than ½ a mile of them.*

This is a study in nonchalance. Having the appearance of being totally unmoved is not necessarily the same as *being* totally unmoved. Imagine the discipline it must have taken to assume such a countenance. This is not a performance like the one witnessed earlier that day on the northern headland, when the two men who had decorated their bodies shook their spears in a 'token of defiance'. But it is a performance nonetheless. The scene being played out on the shore is an ordinary, everyday one. It has not been especially staged for the benefit of the strangers. The locals on the beach are going about their everyday activities as usual, but this time with a kind of self-consciousness that is typical when one is being watched. As this local family prepared their dinner, all its members had to play at being unaffected by the presence of the strange ship nearby.

Out of the miles of shoreline available, Cook chose to make his first landing where the old woman, six small children and four men were gathered. His journal account tells us that he decided to make his approach at that spot in 'the hopes of speaking with them'. Banks was party to this approach, but he hoped (somewhat unrealistically) that the locals would be unperturbed by the landing party's advance. He writes that:

> we set out from the ship intending to land at the place where we saw these people, hoping that as they regarded the ships coming in to the bay so little they would as little regard our landing.

If anyone at all had been fooled by the study in indifference on the shore, it was the captain and his companions. For as soon as they began to row towards the beach, the indifference quickly turned to defiance.

The landing party was made up of about thirty or forty men, by Joseph Banks' calculations, and the entire contingent travelled ashore in two boats. The manuscript version of a log kept by Peter Briscoe, one of two young servants to Banks, says that 'the Captn went onshore in the pinnace'. This was the same boat that Molyneux had taken out earlier in the day to sound the entrance. It was a small boat, able to carry up to about sixteen men in all, including six oarsmen and a coxswain. The other boat taken ashore for the landing was the long boat, which would have carried most of the detachment of marines. There could have been up to twenty men in that bigger boat, if Banks' estimation is to be believed.

The convention covering landings was for one or both boats to remain sufficiently manned and in the water to provide protection for those on shore, if or as the situation demanded. Cook's instructions to the crew was that:

> Upon landing on any unknown coast or Island a sufficient guard is always to be left in the Boat or boats to keep them afloat, the party landed are to keep in one Body unless from circumstances the officer finds it necessary to divide into two one of which is to remain as a reserve both to succer the advanc'd part if attack'd and to secure the communication to the Boats which upon all occasions is to be very carefully attended to.

The marines had been preparing themselves, just in case. Three days before, on the open coast, their officer had put them through their exercises with their small arms. They had made sure that their weapons were working, and practised their drill for using them. The noise of it, and perhaps even the display of it, must have surprised the people on shore had they heard or seen it from afar.

In terms of who precisely, and how many exactly, got out of the boats and went on shore that day, it's impossible to know, although certainly Cook, Solander, Banks and Tupaia did. If family legend is to be believed, then so did a young ordinary seaman called Isaac Smith, the nephew of Mrs Elizabeth Cook, the captain's wife. The story goes that Cook said to young Isaac 'You go first' as they disembarked. The various logs do not help much to fill in the details. One records that the 'captain and passengers' went ashore; another 'the captain and the gentlemen', meaning Joseph Banks, Daniel Solander and others in their retinue; yet another that 'the Captn Mr Banks Dr solander &c with their servants and the detachment of marines landed'; while the remaining accounts take a short cut and simply refer to the 'captain &c'. Only one of the logs, the author of which is unknown, bothers to mention that the marines and the boats' crews were armed, as though that detail was worthy of a mention. It's unique among the ship's records of this episode for stating the obvious.

As the two boats approached, on the shore two local men – one young, one old – swiftly assumed a stance not unlike that of the two men on the northern headland who had brandished their spears at the ship earlier in the day. Wrote Banks,

> As soon as we approached the rocks, two of the men came down upon them, each armd with a lance of about 10 feet long and a short stick which he seemed to handle as if it was a machine to throw the lance.

All of a sudden, the mariners were back to where they started. Two men were standing on the shore shouting at them and showing off their weapons. If, before making an attempt to land, Cook had nursed hopes that there were two distinct types of people among the locals – those who demonstrated *defiance* and those who displayed *disregard* in the presence of strangers – he was now certainly disabused of the notion. Local men, it seemed, were quite capable of assuming both postures.

Notice that it is two men again who make the stand. That detail matters. It's common in descriptions of what the locals did when they came into contact with strangers. Most likely, the combination was the 'headman' of the group (or family) that held this territory and one other able-bodied man from among them who was chosen to accompany the elder. Sometimes the headman and his right-hand man advanced in a welcoming manner, as when Captain Phillip arrived in Botany Bay eighteen years later. That time Phillip approached alone and unarmed, perhaps learning a lesson from Cook's previous experience, and two men on the beach came forward. They pointed him in the direction of water. A few years after that, when Matthew Flinders with George Bass washed up on a beach not far south from this place, two local men greeted them and guided them up the river.

However, the pair's role was not always conciliatory. On the *Endeavour*'s first day in the bay, the two men on the north headland in the morning and the two on the south shore in the afternoon appear to have been trying 'to stem the continued advance of the strangers from the sea' rather than welcoming, guiding or inviting them ashore.

Cook characterised the two men's behaviour on the southern shore as resolute resistance. In his journal he described them as men 'who seemd resolved to oppose our landing'. Perhaps he was absolutely right in his assessment, although we should keep in mind that he wrote this after the event and could have been trying to justify retrospectively the choices he had made in dealing with them. What if he had interpreted their actions not as opposition but as a precursor to a proper meeting? It has been mentioned earlier that these displays of defiance might have been more ceremonial than combative, so the idea is not as far-fetched as it may first seem. It is possible that the stance the men assumed was part of a sequence followed in a meeting between two groups who were strangers to each other. Alternatively, what if Cook had interpreted their actions as a warning that he and his men should pull back and wait a little longer before coming any closer? He could have temporarily retreated at this point. He could have gone back to his ship and waited to see what the locals would do. He might have delayed his advance to see whether or not he would be summoned or approached. Temporary retreat to allow for close observation before making a second attempt at landing was what the Earl of Morton, President of the Royal Society, suggested in a long list of hints he handed Cook before he sailed, to help him in his dealings with the local people he would encounter along the way. The historian Inga Clendinnen says 'the hints have the whiff of the candle about them', meaning they were the product of quiet contemplation at a distance rather than first-hand experience close up, but in this instance the Earl might have been right.

At this particular moment in the encounter between Cook and the local people, the possibilities for what would happen next were still wide open. Nothing was as yet inevitable. Yet Cook seemed reluctant on this occasion to leave the door wide open for long. In his dealings with local people in different places during his first voyage he can sometimes be seen biding his time or allowing the local people to take the lead, initially at least. But there is little evidence of this inclination during his first landfall on the east coast of New Holland. Here he acted quickly and determinedly, trying one method, then another, then another in swift succession to achieve his immediate goal of getting ashore despite the disinclination on the part of the locals to have him come close.

Precedent, and not just predisposition or personality, may help to explain Cook's actions in this instance. His determination to succeed in getting ashore this time may have had something to do with the missed or failed opportunities in the days leading up to this one. It is worth remembering that the *Endeavour* had been hugging the coastline of New Holland for over a week after land had first been sighted much further south at what is now known as Point Hicks. Peppered throughout the short entries Cook made in his journal on that voyage northwards are indications that he had been trying to get ashore almost from the outset. As he sailed along the coast, he was scouting for a place to stop. For instance, after two days with land in sight, he writes about the bay he has named Bateman Bay that 'it seem'd to be but very little shelterd from the sea winds and yet it is the only likely anchoring place I have yet seen upon the coast'. The next day he expresses this desire to get ashore again when he writes about an island (now known as Brush Island) that:

> I was in hopes from its appearance that we should have found shelter for the Ship behind it but when we came to approach it near I did not think that there was even security for a boat to land, but this I believe I should have attempted had not the wind come on shore, after which I did not think it safe to send a boat from the ship as we had a large hollow sea from ye SE rowling in upon the land which beat everywhere very high upon the shore and this we have had sence we came upon the Coast.

'A hollow sea rowling': the language is rich and textured. And so the quest continued. As the *Endeavour* continued northward and one day turned into another and another and another, Cook recorded his want, and his occasional attempts, to get ashore. A couple more days after Brush Island had proved to offer no shelter for the ship, Cook described another promising-looking bay that he called Jervis Bay, but of which he recorded: '[because] we had the wind it was not in my power to look into it'. The winds had not died down. Another bay went by. Another two days passed before, with some anticipation, Cook went so far as to have the pinnace and the yawl hoisted to attempt to land at the place now known as Bulli. It was a failure. The winds made it impossible. (To mark the spot, there was once a plaque cemented to the ground that declared: 'Bulli Where Captain Cook First Attempted Landing in Australia'. Acts attempted as well as those realised are almost equal in stature when it comes to commemorating Cook in Australia.) After the past week, now that Cook had found this sheltered bay he was not going to lose time getting his feet on the ground.

As he attempted to make his first landing in this bay, Cook followed what was by now conventional practice. First, by his own account, he

> orderd the boats to lay upon their oars in order to speake to [the two local men] but this was to little purpose for neither us nor Tupia could understand one word they said.

Banks provides the further detail that the two men on the shore 'calld to us very loud in a harsh sounding language'. Sydney Parkinson made words from these sounds, rendering them in his journal as 'warra warra wai'. He was the only one to do so, although there would be some officers on board the convict transports who believed they heard these very same words when they made their first acquaintance with the local people in this same bay eighteen years later. (Those who shouted at the convict ships may well have been the same men who had shouted out to Cook and his crew.) Banks continues that 'we parleyd with them for about a quarter of an hour, they waving us to be gone, we again signing that we wanted water and meant them no harm'. This simultaneous mime across forty or fifty yards of water would have been a sight to witness.

Signs take on an added burden when there are no shared words. Among his list of hints, the Earl of Morton had also made suggestions for signing with local people in the absence of a common vocabulary. Among them was this one:

> Amicable signs may be made which they could not possibly mistake. — Such as holding up a jug, turning it bottom upwards, to shew them it was empty, then applying it to the lips in the attitude of drinking. — The most stupid from such a token, must immediately comprehend that drink was wanted.

Imagine Banks and others miming this from their boat, with or without props. What the signs for 'we mean you no harm' were, is anyone's guess.

That the two groups had no language in common was disappointing. When Cook had first gone ashore in New Zealand at a place he was to dub Poverty Bay, where he had had trouble controlling the situation with the local Maori, he at least had the advantage that Tupaia, the Ra'iatean man who had joined the voyage in Tahiti after forming a friendship with Banks, could understand what the locals said and could be understood by them. Cook no doubt hoped that Tupaia's language skills extended as far west as the place where he sought to make his first entry into New Holland. But that was not so. Tupaia too was without words. 'The voyage had passed out of the islands in which he counted as a go-between', writes Nicholas Thomas.

When it became clear that this fifteen minutes of parleying was bearing no fruit, Cook explains in his journal that:

> we then threw them some nails beeds &c^a a shore which they took up and seem'd not ill pleased in so much that I thout that they beckon'd to us to come a shore; but in this we were mistaken, for as soon as we put the boat in they again came to oppose us.

By throwing things ashore Cook was not simply offering gifts but was, by his own testimony, seeking the local people's consent to land. In a version of his log, which is held in the British Library in London, Cook states that 'We endeavoured to gain their consent to land by throwing them some nails beeds etc a shore but this had not the desired effect . . .'.

If the words the mariners spoke weren't making any sense to the locals, then likewise neither were the gifts they offered. The gesture of offering things as the means for gaining entry does not appear to have been a language the local people understood. This is not to say that they were not accustomed to the exchange of goods at all; or that gifts were not part of the protocols covering meetings between strangers. What it does say is that the local people were extremely cautious about accepting or even touching the things the strangers offered on this occasion.

Cook was mistaken in his impression that the local men had beckoned him ashore upon receiving the beads. If he were mistaken on this count, then perhaps the men in the sounding boat earlier that day had been also when they believed that the local men had invited them ashore. They had not tested their impressions by accepting the invitation as Cook did now. Yet, instantly, Cook knew he had read the signs wrongly when his renewed advance was met with renewed opposition.

Finally, in his bid to get ashore Cook took recourse to his gun. He did not always like to use it, but he always had the advantage of it as his last word in any situation. His determination to get ashore accelerated this first face-to-face encounter with the local people into a violent episode.

> I fired a musket between the two which had no other effect than to make them retire back where bundles of their darts lay, and one of them took up a stone and threw at us which caused my fireing a second Musquet load with small shott, and although some of the shott struck the man yet it had no other effect than to make him lay hold of a Shield or target to defend himself.

By firing his gun, Cook had 'foreshortened the cultural lesson with a musket-ball', to borrow a line from Greg Dening.

The detail about the bundles of darts is worth noting. Matthew Flinders once commented in his journal about a group of local people he encountered on the far south coast of New South Wales, that 'we could perceive no arms of any kind amongst them; but I knew these people too well not to be assured that their spears were lying ready'. The anthropologist Baldwin Spencer described a meeting between two indigenous groups, strange to each other, that he witnessed outside Alice Springs in 1901. He noted that for 'about half an hour, during which time no notice had apparently been taken of the visitors . . . in reality, the local men had provided themselves with their weapons'. Had the same happened here? The studied indifference at lunchtime had perhaps been a screen for the local men's preparations. They had stashed their spears conveniently close by.

Cook had used his gun instrumentally. He had used it in the hope that it would help him to achieve his immediate aim to get ashore, and to gain control in this situation, which he knew from experience was not always easy to do. It is worth speculating that the chaos that had ensued during his first landfall in New Zealand six months earlier was perhaps still raw in his memory. On that occasion, through carelessness perhaps or a failure of judgment, he had allowed a situation to develop in which his coxswain had killed a local within less than an hour of the landing party getting ashore. The heightened tension this had caused in relations between the locals and the outsiders had not dissipated easily. There would be more violence the following day. It was an experience that had left Cook rattled, but unapologetic. He still put faith in a strong arm to control a situation. As Dening has noted:

> No matter how exercised [Cook] was to carry out the instructions of the Royal Society and navy to treat the [indigenous] peoples with kindliness and humanity, no matter how chagrined he was at the actions of his men, he never discovered how he could moderate the behaviour of others whose systems of social control he could not understand nor use, except by violence.

Echoing this view, Thomas reflects in respect to the first landfall in New Zealand that 'Cook believed that if European mariners were challenged or threatened, the prompt use of force – if need be lethal force – would demonstrate that resistance was futile'. His continued commitment to this belief was evident in this encounter on the east coast of New Holland.

By his own admission he fired his musket at the two local men once, then twice. However, his account of what happened in response to those shots suggests that his weapon's effects were not easy to predict in this place. He used the phrase 'had no other effect than' when explaining what happened after each shot was fired from the boat. It seems that even firearms did not speak a readily recognisable language in this place. 'I fired a musket between the two which *had no other effect than* to make them retire back where bundles of their darts lay and one of them took up a stone and threw at us', wrote Cook of the first shot fired. The reply to the gunshot was a stone. Cook would have to fire again and this time at the body to make his message more plain. 'And although some of the shott struck the man yet it *had no other effect than* to make him lay hold of a Shield or target to defend himself', wrote Cook of the second shot. Once more, 'no other effect than' is the phrase Cook uses to describe the impact of his gun. It is a phrase that indicates the gap between the intended message carried by the small shot and its reception. Rather than a simple cause-and-effect narrative, Cook's account might be more accurately characterised as possessing a 'cause and no other effect' structure. The two shots fired from the boat had neither overpowered nor cowed the two men on the shore. They had stood their ground in the face of them.

This mismatch between cause and effect at the heart of Cook's account is completely absent from the shorthand record of the episode entered into the ship's log and repeated in various other logs that borrowed from it. The ship's log reads:

> Hoisted the boats at 3. The captain, with Mr. Banks and Doctor Sollandr, went on shore. They were oppos'd in attempting to land by some of the natives, who they were oblig'd to sting with small shots, which frighten'd them into the woods.

If only it had been that easy. This was an account so stripped of detail that it became an unreliable record of what happened. When we last saw them, the locals were still standing firm despite one of them, according to Joseph Banks, having been hit in the legs with small shot. And it looked as though they had every intention of remaining at their post on the rocks that bridged sea and land because the wounded man had gone to get a shield to protect himself. This was surely a sign that they were not going anywhere; not yet anyway.

The shield was up at his house. 'On this', writes Banks, 'he ran up to the house about 100 yards distant and soon returned with a shield. In the mean time we had landed on the rock'. It was while the man scurried away to get the shield that the landing party scrambled ashore. Cook's account confirms this. And so it was this momentary gap in defence – rather than the direct impact of the shots he had received, or the men's supposed frightened retreat into the woods, for instance – that allowed Cook and his companions to make their famous first landing. This is a subtle distinction but an important one. Courage, not cowardice, created the clearing that made the landing possible.

The man returned with his shield only to find the strangers standing on the shore. The violence of the encounter momentarily intensified at this close range. 'Emmidiatly after [the man went to get the shield] we landed which we had no sooner done than they throw'd two darts at us, this obliged me to fire a third shott . . .', explains Cook. In his journal Sydney Parkinson claims, perhaps truthfully, perhaps hyperbolically – or perhaps it was a flourish added by his editor – that one of the spears fell between his feet. In his account Joseph Banks increases by one the number of shots fired and the number of spears thrown. Upon landing, he writes, one of the men

> immediately threw a lance at us and the young man another which fell among the thickest of us but hurt nobody; 2 more musquets with small shot were then fir'd at them on which the Eldest threw one more lance . . .

So Cook and Banks disagree about who actually had the last word on the beach that day. This inconsistency registers the confusion of the moment. No matter; the end result was certain. Cook and company had landed.

Always BEGINNING

There is a famous Australian painting of this moment on the beach when the landing party had finally made it ashore. The artist was Emanuel Phillips Fox and it was completed in 1902, just a year after the colonies had federated into the Commonwealth of Australia. Titled *The Landing of Captain Cook at Botany Bay 1770*, it is a monumental painting, and not only in size (Plate 10). In it, Cook and his landing party dominate the scene. They are assembled on the sandy, grassy beach set against a background of blue sea and sombre sky. At the water's edge some sailors drag the landing boat, from which Cook and his small entourage have just disembarked, onto the sand. Nearby, Daniel Solander takes a delicate step onto the dune. The second boat, still full of men, loiters in the water a little distance away. Further off in the background the *Endeavour* is at anchor in the bay. Sartorially splendid, Cook stands in the centre of the painting beneath a billowing, bright red English navy ensign held aloft by a young seaman. Joseph Banks stands shoulder to shoulder with Cook but gestures away from him, pointing to the two local men who are shown faintly in the distance on a rise in front of their gunyahs. One holds a shield in one hand and in the other a spear, which he has raised as though ready to throw it. His companion is also armed with a spear, but appears to cower a little. A trio of seamen at Cook's feet are leading an assault on them. The red-coated marine, his back to the viewer, crouches on one knee with his weapon cocked to his eye taking aim at them. Two sailors with guns in their hands run to assist him. But Cook motions to them to stop where they are. With an outstretched arm, he appears to call an end to the violence on the beach. This episode is over, or so the hand seems to say.

The artist has captured colourfully the moment on the beach when the landing had just been made as described by Cook and Banks in their journals. Yet it is by no means a faithful reconstruction of the recorded event. That was never the artist's intention, nor his function as a painter of history. E. Phillips Fox's painting has more to say than simply 'this is what happened'. By looking closely at the painting, as well as into the story of its creation and circulation, a great deal can be learnt, both about the event it portrays and about that event's status as a revered, foundational moment in Australian history. The painting is a good illustration of the ways in which the confusing, clumsy and violent incident of Cook's first landing on the east coast of the continent could be cleaned up and smoothed out to become a symbolic story of national genesis.

E. Phillips Fox's painting *The Landing of Captain Cook at Botany Bay 1770* was commissioned by the National Gallery of Victoria in Melbourne and was 'intended to honour Federation', which had formally taken place on 1 January 1901. The nature of the commission as a commemoration of the recently formed Commonwealth of Australia is central to the work. Phillips Fox appreciated that Cook's arrival in Australia, which was the theme he had been instructed to paint, was widely considered as a foundational moment in the new nation's history. His assignment was to create a painting that matched the considerable symbolic weight that this past event had begun to carry. Through the careful selection of what scene to paint, in the ways in which he composed the painting's elements, motifs and symbols, in his considerable attention to detail on the one hand and the addition of some clever fanciful flourishes on the other, E. Phillips Fox transformed into grand and noble history the scrappy episode when Cook and his men scrambled ashore. He had painted big history on a big canvas.

While not usually admitted into the canon of Great Australian Art, the painting is nonetheless a pivotal piece in the history of Australian art and in the art of Australian history. It was especially influential during the twentieth century in shaping popular ideas about this past event, not least because it was reproduced so widely. In the 1920s and 1930s the image graced the Australian pound note so that it *was* national currency and *had* national currency. Small reproductions were distributed to schools across the country and hung on assembly hall walls for wide-eyed Australian schoolchildren to look up to. It adorned commemorative stamps and cheap postcards so that it circulated around the country courtesy of the national postal system.

In creating the painting, E. Phillips Fox borrowed ideas and motifs from other history paintings of Cook, but he combined and composed them in such a way as to produce a completely new national picture. Into one frame he brought together diverse ideas about Cook and his place in Australia's history, about relations between Aboriginal and non-Aboriginal people, about histories of British possession and Aboriginal dispossession, and about the nation's past, present and future. By adorning the event of Cook's first landing with powerful and recognisable symbols, and by shrouding it in pathos and sentiment, E. Phillips Fox created a visual narrative – a historical tableau – that tells a story much greater and grander than the story of the landing itself.

CAPTAIN COOK *stepped ashore and . . .*

The Landing of Captain Cook at Botany Bay 1770 presents a larger-than-life visual narrative of the episode on the beach when Cook and his crew had just stepped ashore for the first time, but it does so with compelling realism. The attention to small details is disarming. By all accounts, the artist had gone to some trouble to present the picture as accurately and authentically as possible. He read through Cook's accounts and those belonging to Banks and others about what had happened when the initial landing was made. He made an excursion to the landing place to take measurements and to make some preliminary sketches. He visited an Aboriginal settlement on the shores of Botany Bay and coaxed two men into posing nude for him as studies for the two local men who stood their ground in the face of the advance of the landing party. In London he studied portraits of Daniel Solander, James Cook and Joseph Banks in order to capture their likenesses. He consulted with a naval expert about the uniforms that would have been worn by Cook and his men.

Assiduously pursuing accuracy in historical details is a hallmark of the tradition of history painting, in which the artist had trained in Europe in the late 1880s and early 1890s, and which he applied to this particular commission. But this does not mean that accuracy in all aspects was the aim. History painters composed visual narratives of historic events; they did not merely illustrate or document them. In their practice they were pedantic, but not at the expense of sentiment. They composed their paintings so as to give form to lofty ideals and in order to evoke a devotional response from their audiences, not just to the historical event and figures portrayed but also to the virtues of History in general. This was done by adding various symbolic elements to the historic scene painted and by composing the scene as a tableau. In this respect, the minutiae that mesmerised sometimes masked ingenious inaccuracies or fanciful flourishes, but not so fanciful as to be unbelievable. The highly trained academician E. Phillips Fox expertly used this technique in his Captain Cook picture.

It is not clear when precisely in early 1901 Phillips Fox visited Cook's landing place on the south shore of Botany Bay, but it was certainly before he sailed for England in early March that year. If he had gone there on 7 January he would have witnessed, along with an estimated six thousand other people, a re-enactment of the landing of Lieutenant James Cook at Botany Bay in 1770. This historical performance was part of a program of events celebrating the federation of the Australian colonies, which had formally taken place a week earlier on 1 January 1901. Its inclusion in the federation festivities indicated the importance of the first landing in the new nation's history, and the form it took pre-empts in some respects the preoccupations that were eventually evident in Phillips Fox's finished painting.

In a manner that would become standard practice, the re-enactment presented the first landing as consequential, in both senses of the word. The event was deemed historically important, although not simply in its own right. It was important precisely because it was imagined as leading directly to something else, the something else in this case being the formation of the Australian nation. The formulation was a simple one: *Captain Cook stepped ashore* and the territory became a British possession. *Captain Cook stepped ashore* and history began in this place. *Captain Cook stepped ashore* and ushered in the British and ushered out the Aborigines. *Captain Cook stepped ashore* and the seeds of a prosperous nation were planted. *Captain Cook stepped ashore* and you fill in the blank. These are, of course, all long bows to draw from this event. The actualities are more mundane. Closer to what actually happened that day was that *Captain Cook stepped ashore* and looked around for water and wood.

In order to weave retrospectively the event of the first landing with later historical developments in the story of the nation, a common technique was to ascribe to Cook and his offsiders visionary powers. Commonly they were portrayed as seeing in their mind's eye the future that would unfold in this place. As the cultural theorist and historian Chris Healy quips: 'To know history in the colonies was, it seems, to know the revelation of the past in the future'. And so in the re-enactment's second act, which began once the landing party had stepped ashore, James Cook, Joseph Banks and Daniel Solander played their parts as history's soothsayers. They had exclusive use of the stage (the shore) to deliver the speeches especially written for them for this performance. Their speeches were prophecies. It was at this juncture between the opening act and the closing one that the performance shifted from straightforward historical reconstruction based on the historical record to allegory, in which Cook et al. acquired 'luminous vision' and 'prescient anticipation' of the future.

Predictably, in this little drama Cook spoke first. He forecast future greatness for this land he claimed to have discovered.

> *Within this land shall prosperous nations dwell / And Cities rise to splendid power and wealth, / With dome and tower, with palaces and streets / Of myriad homes.*

Joseph Banks was next. His speech celebrated the Science that had brought the Endeavour to the place and praised the country's natural beauty and abundance. At Cook's prompting, he assessed the country as suitable for future colonisation.

> *Along these shores shall gardens rich appear; — / These marshy lands a golden harvest bear, / And meadows broad and pasturage abound / For herds and flocks throughout yon spreading plains: / So, countless populations here may dwell, / And in the distant days their cities build!*

Daniel Solander spoke last. He expressed collective pity for the two local men who had opposed the group as they made their landing:

> *Our hearts were filled with pity at the sight / Of those poor, dusky savages who sought / But now so bravely to defend their Land / 'Gainst our invading steps*

but concluded by naturalising the violence that the landing party had used against them. The local people's defeat was inevitable and even preordained, he suggested.

> *As shadows flee before the dawn of day / So the dark tribes of Earth in terror flee / Before the white man's ever onward tread; / and all the night of ignorance and sin / Doth vanish as the light of Truth's fair day / Dawns in the East and spreads o'er all the Earth!*

This is how it would be, always and everywhere, Daniel Solander seemed to say. No matter how brave the local people, their defeat was certain. This explanation serves as an apologia for violence – not only in this encounter but also throughout the long nineteenth century of Australian colonial frontiers – that began with the establishment of the penal colony at Port Jackson in 1788 and continued from that time on. Although Solander belongs to a time before British colonisation in Australia, his speech sounds like one a colonist would make. *Necessary* was the verdict on the violence, even if regrettable.

Before the performance had got to this stage, the audience had been entertained with a long and dramatic prelude. The cast, which included a group of Aboriginal people brought especially from Queensland, acted out the first landing. The scene began with the local people cooking their dinner on the beach as Joseph Banks had observed them and ended with Cook and his men scrambling ashore. All effort was made to stage the scene with as much verisimilitude as possible, with only a flourish or two for dramatic effect, such as a dance by the local people while they waited for their fish to fry. The segue to the next act was the wounding of one of the two local men with small shot, upon which (according to the program notes) they retreated, 'leaving the coast clear for a landing, which Cook and his party then effect to appropriate music'. This was an abridged version of events, in that the violent showdown on the beach appears to have been excised from the script. Historically, the two local men had *not* departed before the landing was made. But in this reconstructed drama, the Aboriginal people from Queensland had played their part as per the stage directions that had been written for them. They had been present in the opening act in order to become absent in the closing one. They went quietly.

ONCE WERE *warriors*

The idea that the two local men had been forced to retreat when (or even before) the landing party got ashore, or that their eventual departure from the beach was clear evidence that they had been defeated by the advancing landing party, is a very popular theme in twentieth-century Australian visual and textual treatments of Cook's first landing. This interpretation is expressed by E. Phillips Fox in his painting by putting the two local men in the background of the picture and on the margins of the canvas. In this position, they are portrayed as almost defeated. The contest between the British mariners and the local men is all but over.

Yet this interpretation gains ground only in the late nineteenth and early twentieth centuries. In general, that was not the way in which the two local men were usually portrayed in earlier nineteenth-century illustrations of Cook's first landing. More commonly, they were shown as attempting to keep the advancing party at bay. With one or two notable exceptions, Cook and his landing party are shown in these earlier images as still at sea – in the two boats approaching the shore – while the two men hold their position on the beach. These images are typically composed on a single plane, in which the two opposing sides face each other square on. The mariners and the locals are illustrated as identical in size, although uneven in number. For instance, in an etching published in an early Australian history book in 1865, the two local men are pictured standing stoically on the beach with their weapons raised as the landing boats approach (Plate 7). In a quite rare touch, in the illustration a marine in the bow of the lead boat points his gun at them. This image was printed alongside an extract from Hawkesworth's edition of Cook's journal describing the first landing. Seven years later, in 1872 – only two years after the first centenary of Cook's arrival in Australia – the two men are illustrated again in an image portraying the same scene (Plate 9). Their stance remains the same, but in this rendition Cook is shown seeking to appease them by offering gifts.

In their composition, these nineteenth-century Australian images of Cook's first landing at Botany Bay roughly imitate the models that had been established by late eighteenth-century history painters in Britain who created illustrations to accompany the text in Cook's published voyage journals. The best-known examples can be found in the earliest published account of Cook's second voyage, which contained four illustrations of landings including *The Landing at Erramanga, one of the New Hebrides* (Plate 6) and *The Landing at Mallicolo, one of the New Hebrides* (Plate 8). These are not scenes simply taken from life. The art historian Bernard Smith revealed that the figures in *The Landing at Erramanga* were created by G. B. Cipriani, 'one of the best known history-painters in England at the time', and not by the artist William Hodges, who was on the second voyage. They are later visual reconstructions of events that had been described in words.

In these late eighteenth-century illustrations, as in the Australian images that imitated them, the local people are drawn within their own environment. They occupy the country. In the Australian images they are portrayed on a narrow beach in front of a cliff face, which is very like the actual landscape around where the landing took place. The voyagers are also illustrated in their 'natural' environment – on the water in a boat. The two sides to the encounter face each other in this moment of meeting. In the Australian images of Cook's first landing at Botany Bay, the event was portrayed sometimes with an emphasis upon Cook's attempts at appeasement (as in the 1872 image) and at others with his use of violent force (as in the 1865 image), depending on what the illustrator or his publisher deemed appropriate.

Yet, while the pose given to Cook and his men alters from image to image, the stance of the two local men remains fairly constant. They are shown in no other pose than an oppositional and resistant one. The constant presence of the two local men in their unchanging position on the beach facing the advancing party and in their defensive, warrior-like pose captures a common nineteenth-century (or colonial as opposed to national) interpretation of this past encounter, in which the first landing of Cook and his men on the shore is cast as a standoff between two opposing sides. One might argue that this represents an interpretation of this pre-colonial episode through the veil of later colonial experiences, in which relations between local people and colonists were interpreted by and large as conflictual.

The model for the two local men on the shore that would be recycled again and again in nineteenth-century images of the landing emerged soon after the *Endeavour* returned to England in 1771. When the voyage journal of the artist Sydney Parkinson was published posthumously in 1773, accompanying his description of the landing was a plate that carried the title: *Two of the Natives of New Holland, Advancing to Combat* (Plate 5). The plate was prepared by the etcher Thomas Chambers, and in it the two figures are pictured as classical warriors prepared for conflict. The title printed underneath it reinforces this.

Thomas Chambers' rendition of *Two of the Natives of New Holland* has little in common with Sydney Parkinson's rough field sketches of two local indigenous men, which he made while he was at Botany Bay and which is the more accurate rendition of the two illustrations. As Bernard Smith has noted, the two figures depicted in the engraving are more likely to 'owe their stance and posture to the engraver Thomas Chambers and not to Sydney Parkinson' because 'none of Parkinson's surviving field drawings resort to the vocabulary of postures provided by classical statuary for presenting full-length figures'. As this example demonstrates, it rarely takes much time before the products of a cross-cultural encounter become skewed as they are recycled and repackaged for armchair travellers and others. Yet it is Chambers' etching that became the model upon which later nineteenth-century Australian portrayals of the two men were largely based.

Chambers was not alone in draping these figures with classical allusions. His imagining of the two men as classical warriors corresponds with the description of them in the heavily edited version of Cook's journal account, which was also first published in 1773. Cook distanced himself from the publication because he was displeased with the ways in which the editor, John Hawkesworth, had doctored his prose. Through subtle but significant changes to language, Hawkesworth had modified Cook's more matter-of-fact account. In the edited version of the journal, the two local men become 'champions' and their courage is expressly admired by Cook. These are both embellishments to Cook's original text. Yet Hawkesworth's edition of Cook's journal was the only version available in Australia until the closing years of the nineteenth century. And throughout that century, the interpretation of the landing as a contest between two unevenly matched sides reigned.

Captain Cook's *outstretched arm*

When Cook's first landing becomes the subject of E. Phillips Fox's history painting in the opening years of the twentieth century, the contest is portrayed as all but over. In his new painting, Phillips Fox eschewed the model of the two local men as 'warriors' recycled from late eighteenth-century images, and instead chose to base the figures in his painting on two Aboriginal men living on the edges of white settlement, segregated on a tiny pocket of land reserved for the use of Aborigines. His models were not classical warriors but colonised men. He gave them the pose of the 'warriors' but not the physique. It's a small point, but it speaks volumes about the way in which he interpreted in visual language this original encounter.

The literary theorist Anne Brewster argues that E. Phillips Fox's painting is composed to make it look as though the first landing enacts a complete break with the past. In Brewster's view, the painting 'establishes an Australian beginning demarcated by two pasts'. The first rupture is with imperial time (which is the time of Cook and his voyage) symbolised by the Endeavour, which is pictured in the background. The second rupture is with indigenous time, personified by the two local men, who (on the same plane as the ship) are small, shadowy figures on the edge of the large canvas. Compared with the landing party in the foreground, the two men are miniaturised to matchstick size. In Brewster's view, Cook has turned away from these parallel pasts and is instead 'oriented towards the unseen future, the modern nation, and towards us, the viewers of this historical moment'.

If Cook is oriented outwards towards an audience, then it also seems that he is clearing the ground between himself and those who look (up) at him. The gesture of the outstretched arm that Cook makes towards the trio of armed men before him is a remarkable feature of the painting. It's an imagined gesture, of course. There is nothing in the historical records – which the artist had faithfully consulted – that indicates that Cook called a halt to the violence by extending his arm towards his men. By Cook's own account, he had a gun in his hand that day and on the beach had probably fired the final shot.

However, if the gesture cannot be found in Cook's own account of what happened, it is commonplace in images of Cook that were produced in the late eighteenth century and throughout the nineteenth. It's particularly prominent in images that show Cook and his men embroiled in a violent confrontation with local people on beaches around the Pacific during his three voyages. Nicholas Thomas is more specific. He suggests that E. Phillips Fox had borrowed the gesture from John Webber's 1783 painting of the death of Cook (Plate 11). In it, the figure of Cook is shown holding his arm up, commanding his men to hold their fire even as he is about to be stabbed in the back.

Even before E. Phillips Fox used it, the gesture had found its way into at least one late nineteenth-century picture of Cook's first landing at Botany Bay. In one of the first images to show Cook and his landing party already on the beach, an image that appeared in the *Australian Pictorial Almanac* in 1880, Cook holds up his arm in a conciliatory gesture as the two local men continue to oppose him and his men with ferocious gusto (Plate 13). They remain resolute warriors while he has somehow become the peacemaker.

And so, for all its realism, E. Phillips Fox's painting is a largely imagined scene that hangs upon Cook's outstretched arm. The artist uses the gesture to evoke a humanitarian thread that runs through the painting's narrative. In this posture, the unarmed Cook is portrayed as not so much responsible for the violence against the local men as for its conclusion. He is responsible not for the shooting but for bringing it to an end. And he appears to settle the matter of Aboriginal opposition to the incursion of white men into their country as though once and for all.

Yet the trace of violence remains in the painting nonetheless. It has not been completely airbrushed away. Indeed, the genius of the painting lies precisely in the way in which the artist portrays the violence that is clearly recorded in the voyage accounts, but at the very same time cancels it out by portraying Cook as charitably containing it. By means of the imagined outstretched arm, the artist cleverly depicts Cook as both conqueror and conciliator, or as charitable conqueror. This is a story for the new nation at the start of the twentieth century.

We might say that in the painting the artist has put the violence to the side and pushed the two Aboriginal men to the margins. Certainly, the dramatic tension in the artwork derives less from the struggle between the landing party and the local men. The more resonant and redolent tussle is between Cook and Banks. Although they stand shoulder to shoulder in the painting, their bodies are oriented in opposing directions. With desperation on his youthful face, Joseph Banks looks pleadingly towards Cook as though trying to convince him of the threat posed by the two local men in the distance. This references the journal accounts in which Cook mentions that Banks believed that the local people's spears might have been poisoned, which caused Cook (by his own account) to proceed cautiously. But the appeal is ignored. Pointing away from Banks, Cook commands his men not to shoot. He has the upper hand in this tussle, a tussle that is about the 'right' way to deal with Aboriginal resistance to colonial incursion. Read symbolically, the struggle embodied by the opposing signs made by Cook and Banks is the struggle between those who would champion the need for violence against Aboriginal people and those who would oppose it or curtail it. These two figures are made to symbolise the two sides of a debate that continued to run through settler society before and during the period when the artist composed his painting. As with the making of all foundational myths, the artist has dressed this past event in the clothes of contemporary concerns.

Yet some critics who saw the painting when it was first exhibited strongly believed that portraying Cook as even this close to unseemly violence was inappropriate for a national historical picture. When the painting first went on public exhibition in Melbourne in 1902, one commentator thought that the artist had overstepped the mark by presenting violence at all. 'Objection', he wrote, 'must... be taken, both from a dramatic and sentimental standpoint, against Mr Fox's adoption of this mere casual incident as the leading motive of the scene'. A mere casual incident? Not according to Cook. His journal suggests that it was one of the most dramatic moments in all that happened that day. 'It is not well', the commentator continued in his newspaper column in 1902, 'for young Australians to look upon Cook's landing as a shooting down of helpless aboriginals'. And that was his key criticism. His concern was not with the faithfulness or otherwise of the painting to the past event, or at least the description of it recorded by Cook in his journal, but with the way that historic event was presented and interpreted at the start of the twentieth century, when the Australian nation was new. The issue was the image of Cook as a founding figure and the portrayal of the first landing as a founding event. Helpfully, the writer suggested that it would have been much more preferable to show Cook offering beads and trinkets to the local people in a peaceable manner. Appeasement, not aggression. Valour, not violence. That was his preferred model for a new narrative of national origins.

Under the *English ensign*

If Cook's outstretched arm is an artistic flourish, then so too is the large billowing flag flying above his head. It's unlikely that such a large ensign would have been carried ashore during this confusing moment, when Cook and his men were embroiled in an altercation with the local people in their desperate bid to get ashore. Yet, when looking at the painting, it seems perfectly plausible that Cook should stand on the beach under the English ensign. All he did, one imagines, he did under that sign.

Once again, E. Phillips Fox appears to have been inspired by the idea from an earlier painting. This time it's a celebrated history painting by the colonial artist John Alexander Gilfillan, which was completed some time in the 1850s and which the artist presented to the Royal Society in Melbourne in 1859 (Plate 12). Very likely, E. Phillips Fox had seen the painting in Melbourne before he left for England in 1901.

In Gilfillan's painting, Cook is in the process of performing a possession ceremony. He stands in the centre of a small gathering of men, with two of his officers to one side and Joseph Banks to the other with Daniel Solander a little further behind. Also on that side is Tupaia, the Ra'iatean priest. Oddly, he's wearing a yellow jacket and has been given the task of holding the drinks for a toast. Over their heads, a crewman waves a large flag on a long pole. This is the element that E. Phillips Fox repeats in his painting of Cook's first landing.

As Cook's journal account records, he did indeed perform a possession ceremony like the one portrayed in Gilfillan's painting on an island off the far north coast of the continent as he was preparing to leave the eastern coastline for the last time. But that was months after he had landed at Botany Bay. Describing the hastily performed ceremony on an island off the north coast, Cook records in his journal:

> I now once more hoisted English Coulers and in the Name of His Majesty King George the Third took possession of the whole Eastern Coast from the above Latitude [38° South] down to this place by the name of New South Wales, together with all the Bays, Harbours Rivers and Islands situate upon said coast, after which we fired three Volleys of small Arms which were Answered by the like number from the ship.

Then, rather than partake in a feast as Gilfillan's painting suggests, he and his men hurried back on board the ship to avoid the low tide. Cook called the island Possession Island.

The precise location for the scene portrayed in Gilfillan's painting is not specified in any of the titles that have been given to it at different times. Originally known in the nineteenth century as *Captain Cook Taking Possession of New South Wales on Behalf of the British Crown in 1770*, during the twentieth century reproductions of it commonly carried the title *Captain Cook Taking Possession of the Australian Continent on Behalf of the British Crown in 1770*. His claim of possession had expanded from the east coast to take in the entire continent. The version that I have on a greeting card produced by Australia Post has the title: *Captain Cook Taking Possession at Botany Bay, 1770*. However, Cook did not perform a formal possession ceremony like this while he was at Botany Bay, despite the general impression to the contrary. (One might also point out that Cook had not earned the rank of Captain at the time either, so that too is a misnomer in the painting's title.) The blame for this misapprehension lies with re-enactors, commemorators and illustrators. The re-enactment staged in 1901 as part of the federation festivities culminated in Cook performing a formal ceremony of possession. The organisers confessed to the contrivance. 'A certain amount of poetic licence has been taken in regard to the formal act of taking possession, which in reality occurred some weeks after leaving Botany Bay', they declared in the program notes. Others have been less candid since. Yet the close association between Cook landing for the first time and the continent becoming a British acquisition did not necessarily depend upon having the character playing Cook making any solemn declaration. These two separate 'actions' – landing for the first time and claiming possession – were often conflated in the minds of most Australians. Captain Cook stepped ashore and Australia became a British possession, or so the story went.

This popular idea is embedded in a long and complex history of the ways in which the claim of first discovery, the act of first landing and the declaration of possession of the territory were understood in arguments between competing European nations about their sovereignty or otherwise over colonies throughout the world. However, its significance really lies in the ways in which settler nations like Australia use the notion of a single act of possession by declaration to justify or to explain how they got the land. It's a neat fiction, which allows the more thorny matter of the intense struggle between original inhabitants and colonists over land to be sidestepped in the historical narratives that underwrite those settler nations.

In his painting, E. Phillips Fox portrays the act of landing as an act of possession by including the big red flag as a central symbolic element. With the prominence of the pennant as the sign under which Cook stands on the shore, the artist cleverly makes the act of landing equivalent to a formal possession ceremony. In the place of pomp, he produces a symbol. Once more, he has found an ingenious artistic device to make this scrappy event seem like grand history and, once again, he has proved himself an accomplished history painter.

The placement of the flag and the direction in which it flies carries meaning. It billows towards the men who will play a part in the later colonisation of the country, especially Joseph Banks, who will eventually recommend this sandy spot for a penal colony, and the marine who represents the men who will subsequently oversee that settlement. The two local men are beyond reach of the ensign's spread. They do not stand under the sign of the British. This is an unambiguous visual statement about who belongs and who does not to the newly federated national community that the painting has been especially commissioned to celebrate. In this vision of the nation there is no place for Aboriginal people, a fact enshrined in their exclusion from the Australian Constitution, the new nation's foundational document.

The theme of possession symbolised by the flag is reinforced in the painting by the physical presence of Cook and company. They occupy the entire foreground of the painting and almost all the space of the canvas.

Possession depends not only on declaration but also on occupation. More than this, the presence of the landing party is shown as having pushed away the local inhabitants. Possession and dispossession are intertwined in this history picture. As Chris Healy puts it: 'He who in dispossessing indigenous people had possessed the land "first" called forth the new act of national possession'.

In E. Phillips Fox's painting, the depiction of the causes of the local people's dispossession is slightly ambiguous. The two local men are portrayed as though simply slipping from view. By means of Cook's outstretched arm, and because the gun is shielded from view behind the redcoat's back, the role that violence plays in the history of the demise of indigenous people is visually minimised. It's as though Cook is saying that the violence is unnecessary; the local people will go away regardless. The increasingly accepted view in Australia by the time Phillips Fox created his painting was that Aboriginal people would disappear over time, as was shown by Daniel Solander's speech in the 1901 re-enactment. From the little we know about his personal views on the matter, E. Phillips Fox, like many of his contemporaries, appears to have accepted the racialist idea that the Aboriginal population's decline was inevitable.

In this respect, the painting presents the founding moment in the history of Australia as a singular moment of transition. The British arrive and the local people leave. One presence replaces the other. The event of the landing of Cook at Botany Bay in 1770 is a useful device to express this way of thinking about Australia's history because something vaguely like that happened on the beach that day. The landing party assembled themselves on the shore and some time soon afterwards the two local men made their departure from the scene. But when that event is turned into a foundational moment, their departure on that day is made to look as though it is a final act.

The constant retelling of the story of the first landing has overshadowed the rest of Cook's time at Botany Bay in 1770. Repeatedly ending the story at the point at which the local men made their departure makes it seem as though that was the first *and* last that Cook and his crew saw of them. But that was not so. As the voyager journal accounts show, the departure of the two local men on the first day was not the end of them. They were present in the days that followed. By shadowing Cook and his men around the place in the coming days, we can gain a greater appreciation of the nature of the local people's efforts to deal with the outsiders as the two groups temporarily coexisted in the littoral landscape. But for now there is a little more to say about what Cook and his men did once they momentarily had the beach to themselves.

The FIRST DAY *continued*

The journal accounts disagree about the manner in which the two local men finally left the beach after throwing their spears. Some say they wandered away slowly. Others say that they ran for their lives. Cook fleetingly entertained the idea of kidnapping one of the two men. He notes that they left

> but not in such haste but what we might have taken one, but Mr Banks being of opinion that the darts were poisoned, made me cautious how I advanced into the woods.

Cook might have been overestimating his ability on this score. It is not clear he would have caught one had he tried. Nonetheless, his comment confirms that it was always an option he considered using in these situations.

Prior to this landfall, Cook had last kidnapped some locals during that confusing and chaotic first landfall in New Zealand six months earlier, but with very mixed results. In an attempt to open up an intercourse with the local people there, and in the wake of the violence that had attended the first interactions with them, Cook resolved to 'if possible surprise some of the natives and to take them on board and by good treatment and presents endeavour to gain their friendship'. Surprise them he did, but in order to pluck a few of them from their canoes Cook ended up killing a few more. This was a kidnap plan gone wrong. Cook did eventually manage to entertain three local men on board his ship, whom he describes as enjoying themselves, but he concluded his daily account by writing: 'Thus ended the most disagreeable day My life has yet seen, black be the mark for it and heaven send that such may never return to embitter future reflection.' If that black mark still hung over that day half a year earlier, then this may explain why he so easily abandoned the idea of using kidnapping, perhaps with force, during his first landfall on the east coast of New Holland in a bid to make contact with the people in this place. Or he might simply have thought that there would be time enough to try the tactic later, if necessary.

Once the two local men had left the beach, the landing party gathered themselves together and spent some time looking around. They first went up to the local people's village where, Cook explains,

> we found here a few Small hutts made of the bark of trees in one of which were four or five small children with whome we left some strings of beeds &ca.

These were no doubt the same young children that Banks had earlier described in his depiction of the scene on shore in the middle of the day. His account explains that they found 'the children hid behind the shield and a piece of bark', suggesting that the shield they hid behind was the one that the man had earlier grabbed from one of the houses to defend himself. He doesn't say so in his journal entry for this day, but it seems that he or some other member of the expedition took it, either on this occasion or another. Later in his journal, when the Endeavour had at last left the east coast and was sailing towards New Guinea, Banks sat down to write lengthily about all he had seen and experienced during the four months the expedition had travelled from the far south coast to the far north coast. In a short section on weapons, he mentioned the shield again.

> Defensive weapons we saw only in Sting-Rays bay [i.e. this bay] and there only a single instance — a man who attempted to oppose our landing came down to the Beach with a shield of an oblong shape about 3 feet long and 1½ broad made of the bark of a tree; this he left behind when he ran away and we found upon taking it up that it plainly had been piercd through with a single pointed lance near the center.

At the British Museum in London there is a bark shield that fits this description on display in a glass cabinet (Plate 16). It can be found in Case 96 in the Enlightenment Gallery, which used to be King George III's library. It's a great lump of a thing, its size, its rough surface and its lack of adornment accentuated by the delicate, smooth and intricately carved greenstone tikis, whalebone paddles and wooden headrests, footrests and feeding funnels from New Zealand and other parts of the Pacific on display in the glass cases above and alongside it. There is something simple and solid about the shield. It wears upon its surface the marks left by projectiles deflected and lodged. The hole that Banks describes as being made by the single point of a spear sits near to its centre. The hole can be interpreted as evidence of the object's previous use, and its efficacy. A spear had been thrown at it at some time and had penetrated it, but not presumably the body of the man who had held it. On that occasion its owner must have been thankful for it. It is a shield well used, and perhaps particularly well liked, by the man to whom it had once belonged. The dents and scratches preserved on its surface are clues to its biography, in the same way that scars on skin recall scraps and skirmishes.

The story about its use against the small shot fired by Cook or one of his offsiders in 1770 is printed in abbreviated form on the caption card that accompanies it in the British Museum, so that the shield is presented to the public not simply as an example of an object type but as part of (or as participant in) an actual encounter. This sets it apart from the other things on display in the glass cases adjacent to it. The shield is unique among them for having a *known* story attached to it. And so it's an object with a place in a particular history.

On Sydney Parkinson's page of drawings made at Botany Bay in 1770 are the faint outlines of a shield, perhaps back and front, and one of the two local men sketched along the bottom of the page is holding against his lower torso a shield that resembles this one (Plate 4). A year later in England, John Frederick Miller was commissioned to draw some objects brought back on the *Endeavour*, including a few items from New Holland. On a page of illustrations can be found a shield with the same slightly asymmetrical shape as the one on display at the British Museum (Plate 14). Experts believe that Miller must have had the object in front of him in order to have drawn it so precisely.

Looking at the shield provoked me, in ways that the various written descriptions of the landing had not, to wonder about what motivated the local man to run back to get it from his hut, which was estimated by Banks to be a hundred yards away. Did his desire to have it with him say something about the way in which he was interpreting the assault from the strangers on the sea upon himself and his companion? Does his action perhaps suggest that he interpreted the incident as a possible ritual spearing, in which he had the right to defend himself? Or was the shield one of the accoutrements that communicated his status as leader among his people? Or was his retrieval of it simply evidence of the very human impulse to protect oneself against assault? That he did not throw his spear until he had retrieved his shield is a detail worth pondering.

The shield is not the only object to have made its way back to England in the wake of this encounter in late April 1770. Before leaving the village the mariners removed 'all the lances which we could find about the houses, amounting in number to forty or fifty', explains Banks. What would the implication of the confiscation of the spears have been, particularly given that upon examination Banks confirmed that they were for fishing rather than for fending off aggressors? The spears were

> of various lenghs, from 15 to 6 feet in lengh; both those which were thrown at us and all we found except one had 4 prongs headed with very sharp fish bones, which were besmeard with a green colourd gum that at first gave me some suspicions of Poison.... Upon examining the lances we had taken from them we found that the very most of them had been usd in striking fish, at least we concluded so from sea weed which was found stuck in among the four prongs.

It is not clear that this prompted Banks to return them. One wonders whether the locals had surplus enough to compensate for this reduction in the number of spears in their kit.

Of the cache of forty or fifty spears collected that day, and to which were added others souvenired in the following days, and many weeks later during the longer stopover at Endeavour River on the far north coast, four are known with certainty to have survived (Plate 15). They are held in the Cambridge Museum of Archaeology and Anthropology, three wrapped carefully in tissue paper in a long plywood box and the fourth suspended in a glass cabinet as part of a display of Australian Aboriginal material culture. Their provenance to Cook's first voyage and his time on the east coast of New Holland in 1770 is watertight. They came to Cambridge University via the Earl of Sandwich, Cook's patron and occasional first Lord of the Admiralty. In 1771 Sandwich gave the spears, along with other objects collected from other places during Cook's first voyage, to Trinity College Cambridge, his alma mater. For almost a hundred and fifty years, these things were preserved in a cabinet of curiosities (a *wunderkammer*) in the Wren

THE FIRST DAY CONTINUED

Library. In 1914 they were placed on deposit with the Cambridge Museum of Archaeology and Anthropology, where they can now be seen.

On close inspection, the spears are straightforwardly functional and surprisingly sturdy. They have long, thin and slightly crooked shafts, although a couple seem to have been chopped at one end to be made shorter – to fit into the wunderkammer, perhaps? The string, made from natural fibres and wrapped to bind the shaft to the prongs, is beginning to unravel, but only in places. The resin that adds support to the binding, liberally applied, remains fairly firmly in place. But only a few of the fingernail-like fish barbs attached to the finger-like prongs have survived; all the others have fallen off and become lost at some point during the spears' unusually long life. Of the four spears, only one is four-pronged. Two are three-pronged and the fourth is single-headed. If Banks' journal account is to be followed to the letter, this means that only one, or at most two, of the spears to survive into the twenty-first century were picked up from the village on the shore of this bay on this day.

Along with a shield in one hand, the local man whom Sydney Parkinson roughly sketched holds aloft with his other hand a spear nestled in a spear-thrower, so that the drawing shows not only the spear itself but also the style of projecting it. On the page of drawings made by John Frederick Miller in 1771, the same page that includes an illustration of the shield, are quite detailed drawings of two spears from New Holland, one with prongs and one with a single head, which is described in the notes as a javelin. Once again, no doubt, Miller was able to make these drawings with the spears brought back to England on the Endeavour in front of him.

In his summary notes about New Holland Banks confirms that pronged spears were for fishing, but concludes that single-headed spears were 'intended to be used against men', which may explain the size and shape of the hole in the shield on display in the British Museum. Banks describes these as the 'most cruel weapons', made cruel by the addition of

> the stings of sting-rays, a large one which servd for the point, and three or 4 smaller tied the contrary way made barbs: or simply of wood made very sharp and smeard thick over with resin into which was stuck many broken bits of sharp shells, so that if such a weapon pierced a man it was many to one that it could not be drawn out without leaving several of those unwelcome guests in the flesh, certain to make the wound ten times more dificult to cure than it otherwise would be.

More prominent than spears on Sydney Parkinson's page of rough drawings are canoes. He has drawn no fewer than four of them on one page, and perhaps even a fifth at the entrance of the hut in the centre of the page, but it is difficult to determine for sure. All are rendered from different angles, but only one of them is manned. He also made a more detailed drawing of a sturdier-looking canoe, also manned, on another page in his sketchbook, although this may be one he saw later on at Endeavour River on the far north coast, where larger-sized vessels were observed. (Parkinson seems to have had a particular interest in watercraft. He made a series of small studies of the Endeavour and its pinnace, yawl and longboat.)

If Parkinson was especially interested in the local people's canoes, Cook was equally unimpressed by them. Of those he saw lying around the shore on this day, he wrote in his journal:

> three Canoes lay upon the beach the worst I think I ever saw. They were about 12 or 14 feet long made of one peice of the bark of a tree drawn or tied up at each end and the middle kept open by means of peices of sticks by way of Thwarts.

As Thomas quips, 'from someone who made a lot of use of boats, this was damning', although he's quick to point out that Cook's comment 'was a particular proposition, not a comment on a race'.

After a short time spent surveying the scene around the shore, looking at the huts, collecting the spears, commenting on the canoes and searching for water in the sand, the landing party returned to their boat and made their way over to the north shore. They went back to the spot where they had seen the people in the morning. 'Here however we found nobody', wrote Banks. After the morning's excitement earlier that day, the people on the north shore had made themselves scarce. 'When we now landed', confirmed Cook, 'there were no body to be seen'. So on the Endeavour's first day in Botany Bay, there were two, not one, 'first' landings, one on the south shore and one on the north. However, it is only the very first landing on the southern shore that was later celebrated as being of national significance.

In a book called *The History of Australian Discovery and Colonisation*, which was published in 1865 and is billed as one of the first Australian history books, one can find the testimony of a group of Aboriginal men who claimed to have been eyewitnesses to the arrival of Cook in 1770. The Aboriginal men's testimony is printed alongside an extract taken from Hawkesworth's edition of Cook's journal, presumably in an attempt to provide a two-sided account of this historical event. The eyewitness account was purportedly collected by

> a gentleman, a native of Sydney, who had frequent opportunities in his youth, in the early part of the present [nineteenth] century, of acquiring information from the Botany Bay blacks, and who always took much interest in all that related to them.

(To clear up any confusion, 'a native of Sydney' meant that he was a white man who had been born in that place.) My guess is that the gentleman in question was Obed West, born in Sydney in 1807, the son of convict parents.

The account came from six old Aboriginal men whose names were Yadyer, Bullmayne, Dolmoik, Kurrul, Bluitt and Potta. (The latter two were brothers.) Their vantage point was the north side of Botany Bay, the side of the bay where the men in the sounding boat early in the morning had come close to the local people. This was the spot to which Cook, Banks and a few others now returned late in the afternoon, after some time spent on the southern shore. The men's testimony begins with their impressions of the ship when it first arrived at the entrance of the bay.

> Yadyer said that on seeing the ship he went down to a corner of the beach, where a portion of the tribe were encamped, and told them what he had seen. They all thereupon went up the hill to look.

On this score it sounds quite like Banks' account, where he describes a group of men gathered on the headland. The account continued:

> Some of them thought the ship was a large bird. But, as the object of their amazement approached the heads of the bay, they came to the conclusion that it was a large canoe with people on board.

It is worth noting that they did not take long to realise that they were being visited by other men, because much later on, particularly in the mid-twentieth century, Australian historians, journalists and novelists will claim that the men who were on shore that day thought the strangers from the sea were supernatural beings. The men's eyewitness account continues with details about what they observed from their northern vantage point when the ship came to anchor in the bay and some of its people disembarked in two boats from it. The first part relates to what the six men observed the mariners do on the southern shore: 'The boats landed at a small gap, where there was a fine run of water'. But then the location of the action shifts to the north shore. In keeping with Cook's and Banks' account, this eyewitness account from the shore continues:

> After staying there some time, the boats came over to the north side of Botany Bay, and landed on the beach at Kooriwal. Three persons then landed from one of the boats; one of these had on his head something like a 'bangalle'.

A note inserted in the text explains that a 'bangalle' is a 'vessel used by the blacks for carrying water, it is made of bark, drawn together at the ends and fastened with thongs, so as to resemble very closely a cocked hat'. The account continues:

> These three men walked along the beach, the boats pulling close to land, till they came to Bumbera Point, half a mile from Kooriwall, due north. The blackfellows made their appearance on the bank above the beach, with spears and wommeras; but made no attempt to throw a spear at the strangers. When the aborigines appeared the second time, two guns were fired from the boats, on which they drew back into the bush. When the three persons who landed came to Bumbera Point, they got into the boat, and after staying there a short time went back to the ship, which was then anchored just outside the Heads. Either that evening or the following morning two boats came up again to the north side at Bumbera Point, and hauled a seine twice, and then returned to the ships.

The account published in the history book concludes with: 'Such is the report of the landing of Captain Cook, as told by the aborigines, about forty years afterwards'. It's a curious account because it contains small details that correspond with Cook's and Banks' descriptions quite closely, but other details that deviate from them. For instance, there is no evidence that Cook fired two shots on the north shore, as the account claims. Likely, the men's narrative conflates aspects of Cook's arrival with the later arrival of the first fleet in January 1788 and the La Pérouse expedition a few days afterwards. Despite discrepancies, the Aboriginal men's testimony has a place in the story about Cook's time at Botany Bay in 1770, not least because it is a reminder (if one is needed) that there were two sides to this encounter and that each side had its own version of what happened, at the time and later on. And it is a reminder also that, even when Cook and Banks claim not to have seen anyone when they landed on the north shore, or indeed during their other peregrinations in this place, it does not mean that they in turn were not seen.

That night, Banks recorded:

many moving lights were seen in different parts of the bay such as we had been usd to see at the Islands; from hence we supposd that the people here strike fish in the same manner.

The people here might have been fishing, or they might have been on the move because of the strange ship in the bay. It is impossible to know.

So ended day one.

In BETWEEN

The SECOND DAY

The second day began early with Cook sending a party of men again to the south shore to find water. On the beach, they dug holes in the sand. Back from the beach, they found a small stream. They returned to the ship and reported their findings. With fresh water found, after breakfast 'we sent some empty casks a shore and a party of men to cut wood', explains Cook. Watering and wooding was commonly done at the same time but 'watering was more involved than the wood-cutting', Ray Parkin reckons. If you need to know anything about life and labour on the ship, I recommend Parkin's meticulous study *H. M. Bark Endeavour: Her Place in Australian History*, which is full of the most amazing information about boats and ropes and sails. It is here that you will learn that the pinnace had three pairs of oars, the yawl two and the longboat four. Small details help conjure up the scene on the shore in the days immediately following the first landing.

With all effort aimed at getting wood and water, a work site was quickly established around the stream on the southern shore. From the vantage point of the waterers, this was a good location not only because it was the best source of fresh water found, but also because it was in direct sight of the ship. This ensured safety. Men on board could come quickly to the waterers' aid, if needed, or the waterers could get swiftly into their boat and row to the safety of the ship. For the locals, the locus of activity was less than desirable. The work was taking place near to their sleeping place and their own water supply, and the spot where they launched their canoes into the water. The newcomers were impinging on their domicile. Out of the entire length of shoreline available to them, the voyagers chose to move into the bit already occupied.

Around the stream some labourers spent time filling the empty casks with water, which they then rolled into the longboat pulled up close to the shore. 'Water in a cask is heavy and awkward', Ray Parkin explains, 'especially off a beach and into a boat. It requires considerable work and experience'. The carpenters were on the shore chopping down trees for wood.

Imagine the busy, noisy scene of men at work. I scan the list of the ship's company to see who might have been among those responsible for filling the casks with water and for cutting down the trees. As cooper, Isaac Johnson made and repaired the casks but it was probably not his job to fill them. Matthew Cox, Alexander Simpson, John Dozey, James Tunley, Thomas Jones, Antonio Ponto, Michael Littleboy, William Peckover, Manoel Periera: these men are all listed as able-bodied seamen. The men listed as carpenters and carpenter's mates are John Satterly, Richard Hughes, George Novell, Edward Terrel, Francis Haite, Samuel Moey and Benjamin Jordon. Perhaps all were on shore this morning to do the grunt work that made voyaging possible.

Joseph Banks, Daniel Solander, James Cook and some others spent the morning looking around the place. First they went to the 'huts' close by, where they had spied the children huddled under cover the afternoon before. They 'found laying about the huts' the trinkets they had left there – 'every individual thing which we had thrown them', Banks writes. Every individual thing. Not one item was missing. They had taken none of the trinkets as though in payment for the seized spears. This was a sign of things to come. The local people did not touch the things that had been left for them in and around the huts on the first day, and they would not touch any other thing belonging to the strangers, either offered to them or left lying about the place, throughout the week that followed.

'Probably the natives were afraid to take them away', Cook speculates. Perhaps they were fearful of the strange things, or of the strangers' things. Maybe they did not like the way the offerings had been made. Or they were suspicious that there might be strings attached to the ribbons and other bibs and bobs they found left lying on the ground. Objects have weight, endowed by people with 'agency, efficacy, and personality of various kinds', as the archaeologist Denis Byrne reminds us. It is likely that the local people did not interpret the strangers' things as inert. Taking these trifles might be dangerous. Or accepting them could initiate a relationship of reciprocity that would be better avoided. These goods had been offered without ceremony. More than the things themselves, that was probably the problem. 'The ceremonial context and the act of exchange were the valued products rather than the objects so exchanged', writes the archaeologist Sandra Bowdler.

The mystery of the motivation of the local people was not all that bothered the mariners. Joseph Banks regrets that they 'found not the least good effect from our present yesterday'. He means that the object offerings had not helped to open up communication with the locals. They were strangers to each other still. In many of the places the voyagers had visited before arriving in this place, the exchange of things had been the language of encounter. (And it would continue to be in the voyages that followed, as the large collections from Captain Cook's three voyages now held in museums around the world attest.)

Yet there was more to things than simply a means to make contact. The historian Bruce Buchan says that Cook was not merely gifting when he left things for the local people on his first day in the bay. He had hoped, rather, to commence trafficking things with them, as this would be the means by which to make sense of their society. 'Indigenous participation in traffick [sic]', Buchan writes, 'was used by Europeans to judge Indigenous political, legal and social structures'. A lively trade on the beach could serve to identify leaders and powerbrokers, and to expose the machinations of local politics. The desire for this information was not disinterested. It potentially provided inroads for making deals, if deals needed to be made. That the voyagers had wanted to begin a traffic in things with the locals is borne out by Joseph Banks' comment in his final observations where he writes:

> These people seemd to have no Idea of traffick nor could we teach them; indeed it seemd that we had no one thing on which they set a value equal to induce them to part with the smallest trifle.

Finding the things still strewn about the place exactly as they had been left was the first piece in what would become a mosaic of material gathered by Joseph Banks and James Cook about the local people's acquisitiveness, or otherwise. When they finally reached the end of their journey along the long east coast of New Holland, James Cook and Joseph Banks sat down separately to write up their observations of the place and its people. Both men devote some space to their views on the New Hollanders' attitudes to things. The topic produced one of Cook's most famous lines, when he wrote:

> From what I have said of the Natives of New-Holland they may appear to some to be the most wretched people upon Earth, but in reality they are far more happier than we Europeans; being wholy unacquainted not only with the superfluous but the necessary Conveniences so much sought after in Europe, they are happy in not knowing the use of them.

Usually a great believer in the accuracy of Captain Cook's observations, John Cawte Beaglehole (an authority on Cook and his voyages) accused the navigator of 'writing nonsense' on this score. Romantic claptrap was the gist of his reaction. Glyndwr Williams (another highly respected Cook scholar) is not so quick to dismiss the sentiment as silly. He argues that Cook's conclusions, which he stresses were based on very slim pickings, were simply imbued with European ideas about 'primitivism' that were in circulation at the time. In Cook's time, possessing little and living happily was a common trope about peoples outside Europe.

The local people's materialism (or lack of it) is the source of a celebrated difference of opinion between James Cook and Joseph Banks. Unlike Cook, Banks stops short of calling the locals happy:

> Thus live these I had almost said happy people, content with little nay almost nothing, Far enough removed from the anxieties attending upon riches, or even the possession of what we Europeans call common necessaries.

In his assessment 'Banks airs the anxieties of an aristocrat', writes Nicholas Thomas. He is unwilling to dismiss so quickly the pleasures of the wealthy existence. No such barrier existed for Cook, it seems. He had lived the more modest life of the two men. Given his background, which had included exposure to Quakerism, 'we might guess', continues Thomas, 'that a little Quaker censoriousness rubbed off on him, and that he did not just notice but approved of people with a paucity of possessions'.

Philosophical ruminations aside, back at the village on the south shore of the bay on the second morning Lieutenant Cook, Mr Banks, Dr Solander and company scanned the scene for clues. 'No signs of the people were to be seen', explains Banks. The local people had left behind evidence of the voyagers' recent presence at the place, but not their own. At this point the

THE SECOND DAY 55

mariners parted company. Banks-the-botanist went to explore the 'woods', although which part of the woods is not clear. Cook-the-charter went to explore the bay. Both probably expected, and certainly hoped, that in the course of their excursions they would come into contact with the local people. But neither party did. Banks tells us that he and Solander 'found many plants, but saw nothing like people'. This is how Joseph Banks' stay in the bay began, and as it began so it continued. Day after day he made acquaintance with many plants, which delighted him, but with no people at all, which disappointed him.

On his peregrination that morning, Cook saw people only from a distance. He records in his journal that when he was in the pinnace sounding and exploring the bay, he

> saw sever[l] of the natives but they all fled at my approach. I landed in two places one of which the people had but just left, as there were small fires and fresh muscles broiling upon them – here likewise lay vast heaps of the largest oyster shells I ever saw.

These vast heaps of shells were the remains not only of the day. They were the remains of days upon days, years upon years, centuries upon centuries, millennia upon millennia. The archaeological estimate of the time of continuous human occupation in these parts is six thousand years. One midden on the southern shore of the bay, which archaeologists excavated in the 1960s, had begun accumulating about two thousand years ago. The middens were still visible in the opening decades of the twentieth century, when they became playgrounds for amateur collectors of things Aboriginal.

Local people fleeing from Cook and leaving behind their still sizzling supper would not be a unique event. Almost every time Cook approached the local people, whether in his boat or on foot, alone or in company, presumably always with a gun in hand, they took to their heels. Whenever I read Cook's many mentions of this phenomenon, I can't help wondering if the local people identified him as the man who had fired at their countrymen on the first day the strange ship was in the bay. His distinctive uniform might have given him away, or his particular stance and stride, or the way he wore his hair.

Some later historical treatments of Cook's arrival on the east coast of New Holland expressed the notion that the local people did not recognise Cook and company as men but as ghosts, or as some type of spirit beings. For instance, when the journalist and historian Keith Willey in 1979 published a history of Aboriginal people living in the region around Sydney, he explained the local people's attitude to the Endeavour in this way.

> The more likely explanation must lie in the enclosed Aboriginal view of one earth, where life was as it always has been, and land and ocean stretched away to meet the rim of the sky. Spirits were all about them and the Endeavour, among a people who conceived no craft larger than bark canoes, must have seemed like a voyager from a place of ghosts.

Attempts like this to see the event through Aboriginal eyes often shrouded the scene with magic and mystery. There is something of this in Eleanor Dark's treatment of the incident in her historical novel The Timeless Land, published in 1941. The character Wunbula, whom she created as the first to see the voyagers arrive, initially believed the Endeavour to be 'a spirit sent by Turong, who rules the water'. Dark later describes it as 'a magic boat', and its crew as 'mysterious beings with faces pale as bones'.

But the reality was most likely more mundane than these treatments suggest. There is little in the local people's behaviour at the bay as recorded by Cook, Banks and the other mariners that approximates to other recorded episodes when it was clear that indigenous people believed the 'white' men they encountered in their country were ghosts or dead kin returned. Often those instances involved a woman identifying a strange white man as the ghost of a deceased relative. Upon recognising him in this way, she typically proceeded to hug and kiss him and to weep demonstratively. During the time that Cook and company were in the bay, no woman approached any of the mariners in this way, or indeed at all. The entire encounter is characterised by the near total absence of women. Rather than spirit beings, it's more than possible that the locals knew that these strangers were men like themselves, and that they simply did not want to meet with them for fear of the consequences. However, that explanation is less exciting than the evocation of enchantment and enrapture.

Back at the watering place near the beach, the wooding and watering work continued until the middle of the day. 'At noon all hands came on board to dinner', reports Cook. The coast was at last clear. 'The Indians, about 12 in number, as soon as they saw our boat put off Came down to the houses', writes Banks. The local people might not have made themselves very visible during the course of the morning as the strangers established themselves on the shore, but the precise timing of this incident makes it obvious they had been keeping an eye on comings and goings. 'Close by [the huts] was our watering place', Banks continues, *at which stood our cask: they lookd at them but did not touch them, their business was merely to take away two of four boats which they had left at the houses; they did this, and hauld the other two above high water mark, and then went away as they came.*

Bereft of spears, they claimed their canoes.

After the midday meal, the men returned to their work. Various logs record that on board the ship the men were employed in the hold, the armourer at his forge and the sailmakers repairing sails. Others went back on shore. Cook and Banks returned to their respective explorations and the wooders and waterers returned to their employments around the stream.

Late in the afternoon around five o'clock, as the labourers on the shore were winding up their work for the day, a group of local men appeared. Sixteen or eighteen of them, according to Cook's account – fifteen, says Banks, and about seventeen, says Lieutenant Hicks, who was actually there – 'came boldly up to within a 100 yards of our watering place and there made a stand'. My guess is that they stood at the top of the low ridge behind the stream where they could be easily seen. If so, they had strategically placed themselves between the country that lay behind them and the sea where the strangers' ship was still at anchor. This stand of local men was no doubt an impressive sight, but what impression it had on the labourers who witnessed it we don't know. We don't have their words, only a short written account from Lieutenant Hicks and slightly more wordy second-hand versions of events based on oral accounts written up by Cook, Banks and others.

That they came *boldly* suggests that the group of local men used definite and distinctive movements as they advanced towards the waterers and wooders and that they travelled in unison. They might have been making a noise as they approached. All were armed with 'darts and wooden swords'. The 'wooden swords' were probably throwing sticks, but the mariners had trouble identifying them. The records don't say so, but I suspect that as they advanced as a group they held their spears and throwing sticks aloft. This is a posture commonly described in accounts written in the early years of the British settlement around Sydney and illustrated by some of the early colonial artists.

The action had been planned. In the interim between yesterday afternoon and this afternoon, the locals had had 'time to assess and discuss the newcomers, and reach a consensus of their own course of action', to borrow a line from Hallam; a course of action that would be adjusted again and again in response to what the strangers did. They were not simply sticking to a script, but were experimenting with possible courses of action drawn from a repertoire. Today they had decided to approach the strangers in a formal and disciplined way. Yet the efficacy of the action would depend partly on the response of the strangers to it.

With the appearance of this party of men on the afternoon of day two, the departure of the two men on the shore the previous day when Cook and company had scrambled ashore no longer looks like a final retreat. They were not so easily overawed by the presence of strange men in their country. They had not been summarily defeated, as much of the subsequent settler storytelling about the event suggests. Yesterday they had not wanted the men from the sea to enter their territory. Today they did not want them to stay in it. They returned boldly to continue to defend their territory, their resources and their kin.

As the local men boldly advanced, the woodcutters and waterers gathered themselves into a group behind Hicks, their officer, and his second in command. It is difficult to know how many men were in the working party that day. They had come ashore in the longboat, so perhaps (at most) there were twenty of them. If so, their number may not have been much greater than the group of local men that faced them. The size of the two sides had evened out compared with the situation the day before. For a short time the two phalanges of men faced each other at a distance apart. Each held their ground in this edgy standoff.

At this juncture, two men from the local group walked slowly forward towards the mariners. It was two again. This is more evidence of a repeating pattern, which would take shape over the following days as incidents like this one recurred. These were the men from among the group whose role it was to invite, intercede, incite or entice. They were the ones who were on this occasion 'empowered to make a formal approach' – envoys, if you like. Zachary Hicks tells us that, as these two men advanced, they 'talkd much in an unknown tongue'.

It is not clear if these two men are the same two who faced the landing party on the first day. None of the journals say so one way or another. However, it's worth remembering that the labourers on the shore that day had not been part of the landing party the day before. Even if the two men were the same, there was no one present who would necessarily recognise them. Generally, the various voyager accounts of the encounter at Botany Bay do not distinguish one local from the next, which is symptomatic of the absence of close contact. Unlike at Endeavour River, where the voyagers were forced to stay longer, they do not learn the name of any one local person; they cannot distinguish one person from another; and none of the voyage artists gets sufficiently close to draw a portrait. Rather than identifiable individuals, the local people around the bay appear in the records as an indistinguishable mass. To be sure, the mariners are adept at counting them. Four in one group they tell us, sixteen this time, twenty-two on some other occasion. They also describe their general appearance – texture of hair, colour of skin, absence of clothes. However, the local men who present themselves time and again to the strangers around the shore are not introduced to the reader as people or personalities.

In response to the two local men walking towards the labourers talking all the time, Lieutenant Hicks and another man stepped forward to meet them. Zachary Hicks was the man who had first spotted the east coast of New Holland as the ship sailed westwards from New Zealand. This was a claim to fame that saw his name immortalised on Cook's chart, when the starting point of the *Endeavour*'s journey along the continent's coastline was called Point Hicks. (His immortality was initially short-lived, because later explorers on that part of the coast overwrote his name on their charts with a new name. He came back to life in 1970 during Cook's bicentenary, when a jagged, windswept precipice on Victoria's eastern coastline was ceremoniously christened Point Hicks.) Like Robert Molyneux, Hicks was on his last voyage, although he didn't know it then. He died from consumption just over a year after this incident by the stream. In fact, he had been dying the entire voyage, or so said Cook. The consumption that killed him was already with him when the ship left England.

Lieutenant Hicks sought to entice the two men 'by offering them presents &ca', but according to Cook 'it was to no purpose'. The mariners relied on old methods. They were yet to learn that giving gifts was not the means by which to start a conversation in this place. There might have been a proper time for making offerings, but this was not it. The thrusting of things towards the two men showed little of the restraint that was required on this occasion. In his defence, Hicks probably did not know that Cook and Banks had that morning found the gifts they had left yesterday lying about untouched at the huts. If he had, he might have tried some other approach.

The two local men had no doubt hoped for a different response from the strangers. If Hicks had gone a bit more slowly, he might have stumbled across what that was. It is possible the two men had stepped forward to invite the strangers to follow them so that a formal meeting could begin.

If this had been the case, Lieutenant Hicks would have done well to organise his men into a solid square and prepare them to march forward in formation. More likely, though, they had come to see the strangers off their country. In writing up the details of this encounter, Cook explained that: 'All they seem'd to want was for us to be gone'. Because the statement appears in his account, Cook is often assumed to be the source for it. But these words are more likely to have come from Hicks' lips when he gave a report to his captain about what had happened. He used similar words when he briefly recorded the episode in his own daily log, which unlike Cook's was not published. There he states that he believed that the purport of the many words that the two men spoke as they advanced was 'either commanding us to go away or daring to single combat'. It's more likely the former than the latter. As the two local men stepped forward towards the party of sailors speaking to them as they did so, they might have also been gesturing to them to go the way they had come. Other accounts of other expeditions describe local people showing voyagers the exit. For instance, when the French expedition under the command of Nicolas Baudin was on the west coast of the continent in the opening year of the nineteenth century, in one incident about 'seven or eight natives' blocked the path of some of his men as they walked into the country from the beach. 'In their gestures', one participant reported, 'they appeared to invite us to retrace our steps'.

Rather than accept the things that Lieutenant Hicks offered them during this earlier episode on the east coast, the two local men and the others behind them 'did not wait for a meeting but gently retired', says Banks in his report of the encounter. The locals had made this choice before. This is what the two local men the day before had done when confronted by Cook and his landing party on the shore. Rather than push the point, on both these occasions the local men left the scene, but not in haste. They retired rather than retreated. And they would do it again and again before the *Endeavour* finally sailed away a week or so later.

It is obvious to say it, but the locals must have been confounded by these strange men. As Sylvia Hallam puts it: 'The European intruders must have caused bewilderment and consternation by totally inappropriate actions and sequences of reactions'. These strangers, we can be confident, were not acting like any strangers the locals had ever met before. They had certainly had dealings with strangers, but those strangers from other parts of the country would have known the drill. These ones did not seem to have a clue. Whether they had had contact with other Europeans is a more controversial matter. There are many who firmly believe (or at least strongly desire) that Cook was not the first European to touch these southern shores. It's an aspect of Australian history that invites seemingly endless speculation but which, the Australian archaeologist John Mulvaney points out, unfortunately suffers from a lack of substantial documentary and material evidence that would help to authenticate any 'certain visits by aliens'. It's foolish to discount the possibility of earlier European contacts on this part of the coast, but the physical evidence, such as deep-buried mahogany ships, or lost keys, or settlement ruins, that is offered as proof of them is highly suspect.

Had there been other contacts on this stretch of coast, they would have happened well before the lifetimes of the people who were dealing with Cook and company on this occasion. They might have inherited stories that would help them to make sense of this encounter, but no personal experience of their own. By and large, they were in a situation with little or no precedent. However, this experience would come in handy when new strangers arrived in large ships eighteen years later. Some of the men in the group that approached the labourers by the stream on this day would be old men by then. Others would have grown from youths to men. All would have memories of this time past.

With the locals having made their retreat, the workmen got into their boats and returned to their ship. As Banks notes, 'our boat was by this time loaded so every body went off in her, and at the same time the Indians went away'. The charged encounter between strangers and locals on day two was over.

In the meantime Cook, Banks and some others were in

> *a Cove on the north side where in 3 or 4 hauls with the saine we caught above 300 pounds weight of fish which [Cook] caused to be equally divided among the Ships Company.*

The equal division, according to almost all the logs, was three pounds each. There was a feast of fresh fish for all on board that night. Banks described them as 'very fine fish, more than all hands could Eat'.

So ended day two.

The THIRD DAY

Day three began noisily. Joseph Banks starts his journal entry this day with the information that:

> before day break this morn the Indians were at the houses abreast of the Ship: they were heard to shout much. At su[n]rise they were seen walking along the beach; we saw them go into the woods where they lighted fires about a mile from us.

Shouting and smoking: these early-morning actions in all probability were directed at dealing with the problem of the ship and its company of unfamiliar men still lying in the bay. Making a loud noise and lighting grass fires were recorded in some early Australian exploration and ethnographic literature as means by which local people sought to deal with unwanted and uninvited strangers in their country. Both, it appears, were deployed as deterrents.

Many were the times local people on the shore shouted at strangers from the sea. When the *Endeavour* first appeared at the entrance of the bay on the first day, the local people who gathered on the headland spoke defiantly. When the first ships of the first fleet arrived at the same place eighteen years later, the people on the headlands shouted at them. When the landing boat from the *Endeavour* carried Cook and the landing party towards the southern shore, the two local men on the shore called very loudly in a harsh-sounding language. When the landing boat carrying Captain Arthur Phillip and his landing party went ashore to search for water for the first time at Botany Bay, the men they saw on the shore 'got up and called to us in a menacing tone'. Once more, comparison with the Baudin expedition on the west coast in 1801 is enlightening. When some men from that expedition approached land in their boat for the first time, the locals on the shore screamed and made a 'great noise'. They approached the strangers coming towards them in a menacing manner, all the while calling out in a 'terrible tone'. Then, on the first night the French mariners stayed on shore, the local people 'continued to howl defiance from the forest'. Early this morning at Botany Bay the local people were in full voice.

'Has anyone paid attention to the sounds of exploration?' the literary theorist Paul Carter asked some years ago. A few people had, although not many because, as Diane Collins argues, most scholars were more interested in examining the ways in which the explorers *saw* the country rather than the ways they *heard* it. When historians and others are attuned to the soundscapes explorers walked through, the emphasis is on natural noises, including the explorers' emotional responses to strange sounds. Did the kookaburras' laugh mock these men who trudged through the bush, for instance, invoking their own uncertainties about the enterprise in which they were engaged?

Among the sounds of exploration are the noises that cross-cultural encounters make. In the opening days of the encounter at the bay, the voyagers heard voices other than their own. They were shouted at and they shouted back. They heard shouting from a distance and they listened. They commented upon the spoken sounds that the local people made, but they could make no sense of them. They failed to identify the meaning of single words and were at a loss to catch the gist of the entire speech. The locals would not shout for the whole time the strangers were in the bay. Later on they would decide that silence was better, but for now they shouted in the hope that the strangers would get the message loud and clear.

What did lighting fires do? It seems to have been a quite common practice among local people in response to uninvited strangers. For instance, when the explorer Charles Sturt was on an expedition along the Macquarie River through western New South Wales in 1828 and 1829, and had on one occasion surprised a group of local men who had been setting a net in a river, the local men's response was to set on fire the bush around the strange party who had suddenly appeared. Sturt writes in his journal,

> We had not long been stationary when we heard a crackling noise in the distance, and it soon became evident that the bush had been fired. It was, however, impossible that we could receive any injury on the narrow ridge upon which we stood, so we waited very patiently to see the end of the affair.

The end, it seems, was that one of the local men eventually approached Sturt and his men. Sturt summarised:

> yet from the extremity of fear that had prompted them to set their woods in flames, they in a brief space so completely subdued those fears as to approach the very beings who had so strongly excited their alarm.

Another illuminating example is described by Cook and Banks, but it is an incident that occurred a few months after they had left Botany Bay. When the *Endeavour* was held up in the winter on the north coast of New Holland (at the place that became known as Endeavour River) after sustaining damage to its hull from the reef, comparatively close relations gradually developed with the local people. Some local men repeatedly came quite near to the ship and accepted food and objects from the mariners, including an old shirt that Cook had presented to a local man. Tupaia played a critical role in getting them to come close by persuading a group to lay down their weapons and to sit with him on the shore.

About a month after the *Endeavour* had been there, relations had developed to such an extent that some local men came aboard the ship. By this time, the mariners had accrued a haul of somewhere between eight and twelve turtles, which lay on the deck. The local visitors attempted (according to Banks) 'by some means or other to get one of our Turtle'. But their request by signs for one was refused, upon which they 'shewd great marks of Resentment'. In response to this refusal, 'they laid hold of a turtle and hauld him forwards towards the side of the ship where their canoe lay'. Some sailors swiftly stopped this initiative. After a couple more unsuccessful attempts to get hold of a turtle in this fashion, the local men hopped into their canoe and rowed ashore. Once there, they took fire from under

> a pitch kettle which was boiling [and] they began to set fire to the grass to windward of the few things we had left ashore with surprising dexterity and quickness.

Banks feared for his tent; Cook for some fishing nets. A small pig burnt to death was the only casualty on the mariners' side. Cook did some firing himself in his usual way, and wounded one of the fire-makers in the process.

On this occasion, the use of fire seems to have been in direct response to something the strangers had done. Possibly, it was a form of retaliation against the strangers for not sharing their catch. Or, perhaps, it was a punishment for taking the turtles in the first place. 'The occasional use of fire against later European explorers', writes Nicholas Thomas, 'suggests that this was a conventional tactic of military harassment in the region'. The matter did not stop with the firing on the shore. Soon after this drama on the beach had come to an end, the local men went away and 'they set the woods on fire about a Mile and a half and two miles from us', Cook explained. But the men returned a couple of hours later, seemingly good friends again.

If shouting loudly on the shore and lighting fires in the woods were part of the local people's attempts at the start of the third day that the *Endeavour* was in Botany Bay to harass the strangers into leaving, then they were opting for methods that did not involve direct confrontation. The strategy here (as on the day before) might have been to 'repel rather than attack'. These are indirect methods of deterrence. They happen at a distance. The paramount principle in such cases is to ensure that, whatever strategy is adopted, it does not lead to lasting bad consequences. The aim in dealings with strangers is to maintain or to restore balance and equilibrium. Strangers were disturbing precisely because 'they threatened the stability and order of the universe'.

Once the day began on shore for the voyagers, Banks and Solander could be found again in the woods collecting specimens. Cook had gone in his boat, this time to 'sound and explore the North side of the bay where', he tells us, 'I neither met with inhabitants or any thing remarkable'. The labourers were at their employments around the stream. Small parties of men were engaged in various activities – one chopping wood, a second collecting water, a third cutting grass. It was business as usual.

As yesterday, a group of local men, about the same in number, approached the labourers. This time they advanced towards the men cutting grass, who according to one report were the farthest away from the rest of the labourers. As yesterday, they were all armed, 'having in their hands sticks that shone (sayed the Sergeant of marines) like a musquet'. This is from the report provided by Joseph Banks. Like Cook's account of the episode the previous day based on the report from Lieutenant Hicks, Banks is reporting what the officer-in-charge, who was probably John Edgecombe, later told him had happened.

Upon seeing the local men approach the grass-cutters, the officer-in-charge gathered all his men together. As the grass-cutters ran to join the others near the watering place, the locals pursued them. 'The haycutters coming to the main body appeard like a flight', writes Banks, 'so the Indians pursued them, however but a very short way, for they never came nearer than just to shout to each other, maybe a furlong'. (A furlong is about two hundred metres.) It's not absolutely clear whether the furlong refers to the distance they ran after them, or the distance they kept from them. What is clear is that the locals were not picking a fight. They pursued them, but only to push them along. The aim of pursuit, it seems, is not to catch the men being chased. The chasing is the end in itself. It is as though they are trying to shoo the strangers away. They encourage them to leave rather than compel them to go. They are still 'refraining from offering any real violence'.

More than this, the local men's actions appear to be directed at getting the labourers to stop what they were doing. Their method once more was to approach boldly, shout loudly and display weapons proudly. They were trying to dissuade the strangers from cutting, chopping and casking the natural resources the country contained, and from staying in their country, and from penetrating any further inland to the tract of country behind the stream. If it was the grass-cutting that perturbed them especially, this was probably because it interfered with their controlled burning practices. This was well-tended country managed mostly by fire, which depended on healthy undergrowth for fuel. The strangers were cutting grass out of season.

Certainly, the early exploration literature is littered with examples of local people seeking to protect their resources from strangers. The turtle incident at Endeavour River is one. Another occurred when William Dampier was on the west coast in early 1688 and the local people worked hard to keep him away from their fish traps. His journal notes that:

> *These poor Creatures have a sort of weapon to defend their ware, or fight with their enemies, if they have any that will interfere with their poor fishery. They did at first endeavour with their weapons to frighten us, who lying ashore deterr'd them from one of their fishing-places. Some of them had wooden swords, others had a sort of lances.*

When the first fleet arrived at Botany Bay in 1788, relations with the local people quickly soured when one of the sailors under instructions from Major Ross began to chop down a tree on the southern shore of Botany Bay. According to another officer, William Bradley, 'the natives were well pleas'd with our people until they began clearing the ground at which they were displeased and wanted them gone'. The phrase 'wanted them gone' has a familiar ring to it.

Back at the same place in April 1770, the locals continued their efforts to repel the strangers. 'At night they came again', Banks briefly mentions, 'in the same manner and acted over again the same half pursuit'. Banks' phrase 'same half pursuit' suggests that he detects an element of performance, or pretence, in their actions. It's like his other earlier phrase, 'a token of defiance'. These are phrases that Banks uses to convey his impression that the locals' actions are decidedly performative. An eye to performance is critical in writing contact history, Paul Carter argues. 'Without a recognition of the theatrical nature of cross-cultural relations in these situations', he writes, 'the very existence of a contact history may be hard to establish'. Banks was a spectator of the locals' performance, but it is unclear whether he was inclined to take any part.

'In the PM', writes Cook, 'ten of the natives again Visited the watering place'. It's not clear if these were the same as the ones who had had a go at the grass-cutters, or the ones that Banks mentions as making the same half pursuit, or a different group altogether. It is sometimes difficult to get Cook's and Banks' journals to correspond with each other. On this occasion, Cook was on board the Endeavour when he saw the ten men visit the watering place in the afternoon of the third day. On seeing them arrive at the stream, Cook quickly hopped in a boat and went ashore, but by the time he arrived they were already going away. They had probably seen him approaching. Nonetheless, he:

> follow'd them alone and unarm'd some distance along the shore but they would not stop until they got farther off than I choose to trust my self; these were arm'd in the same manner as those that came yesterday,

meaning they were carrying spears and spear-throwers. They rarely went anywhere without them. The locals, it seemed, had got away from Cook again.

In the evening, Banks went over to a small island off the northern headland of the bay – now known as Bare Island because Cook had described it as a bare island – where he searched for shells. As he was going there, he saw

> six Indians on the main [land] who shouted to us but ran away into the woods before the boat was within half a mile of them, although she did not even go towards them.

More shouting at the strangers but still, it seems, to no effect. While Joseph Banks was scratching around for shells, a party of seamen was hauling the net for fish. They caught very few. There would be no feast of fish on the ship that night.

At six in the evening, a sailor died from consumption. His name was Forby Sutherland.

So ended day three.

The FOURTH DAY

The fourth day began with a funeral. In the morning, the dead sailor was buried on shore near the watering place. As a memorial, Cook called 'the south point of this Bay after his name'. Presumably, some of the locals witnessed the burial. They had clearly kept an eye on the strangers whenever they were around the stream. This is where they had made their repeated approaches to them. This is where they had come down on the second day to retrieve their canoes as soon as the sailors had gone back to their ship. We cannot know what they thought about this episode. They buried their dead, so the practice itself was not out of the ordinary. But it was no doubt unconventional and perhaps even unacceptable for a stranger to be buried in their territory (and indeed so close to their huts) without their permission or participation.

During the nineteenth century, some colonial poets honoured in hushed and holy tones the sailor's burial on the shore. For Australian poet Henry Kendall, the grave made the ground sacred. In the last stanza in his *Sonnets on the Discovery of Botany Bay by Captain Cook*, which is titled 'Sutherland's Grave', Kendall represents the remains of sailor in the soil as the starting point for a settler (Christian) heritage.

> 'Tis holy ground! The silent silver lights
> And darks undreamed of, falling year by year
> Upon his sleep, in soft Australian nights,
> Are joys enough for him who lieth here
> So sanctified with Rest. We need not rear
> The storied monument o'er such a spot!
> That soul, the first for whom the Christian tear
> Was shed on Austral soil, hath heritage
> Most ample! Let the ages wane with age,
> The grass which clothes this grave shall wither not,
> See yonder quiet lily! Have the blights
> Of many winters left it on a faded tomb?
> Oh, peace! Its fellows, glad with green delights,
> Shall gather round it deep eternal bloom!

An earlier poem by Barron Field, written in 1825, interpreted Sutherland's burial on the shore as proclaiming possession.

>   Close at hand
> Is the clear stream from which [Cook's] vent'rous band
> Refreshed their ship; and thence a little space
> Lies Sutherland, their shipmate; for the sound
> Of Christian burial better did proclaim
> Possession than the flag, in England's name.

The seaman's fame came (retrospectively) from having been the first white man buried on a shore that was subsequently colonised by his countrymen. Within time, the country where he had been buried would be pockmarked with the graves of many other white men. Had he died at sea and his body been disposed of by being thrown overboard, he would have been forgotten by all but his own family and friends. However, his dead body had been left behind in this place, where later it would be strangely interpreted as a holding deposit – a claim to the country until the colonists arrived.

Firsts matter in settler history. When researching his family history, the Aboriginal writer Kim Scott noticed the way in which local historians in particular were obsessed with the 'first white man born' in a place. 'In my research notes', writes Scott, 'I reduced it to the ugly initials, FWMB'. Equally noteworthy was the 'last full blood aborigine', which he shortened to 'LFBA'. The repeated reference to the first white man and the last black man 'seemed to insist on a boundary, a demarcation; the end of an old story, the beginning of a new one – and the concept of race was at the centre of it', he writes. The constant commemoration of the sailor Sutherland as the FWM buried (rather than born) in Australia is part of the phenomenon Scott identifies. A rite of passage in a person's life is used to mark time in a people's history.

After Sutherland's body had been buried, the remainder of the day was given over to exploration. On this day, Cook renewed efforts to make contact with the local people. He first went with a party to the huts 'not far from the watering place where some of the natives are daly seen, here we left several articles such as Cloth, Looking glasses, Combs, Beeds Nails &ca'. Cloth, looking glasses, combs. These were thoughtfully added to the items on offer. They are a superior grade of bargaining chip to the strings of beads and the handfuls of nails that had previously been presented. Cloth in particular had been much desired in other places previously visited. James Cook had raised the stakes.

By leaving yet more things at the local people's village, Cook had not yet given up hope that the local people would want his wares. After three days in the country he still placed his faith in commodities as a conduit for cross-cultural contact. By leaving superior items on day four, he appears to have been operating on the premise that the locals were simply discriminating in their desires. Yet this premise proved mistaken. These newly offered items were treated in exactly the same way as the previous objects had been: they were not touched. No starker contrast with other places previously visited could have been imagined. In Tahiti, gifts were readily accepted and reciprocated, and a lively barter had developed with food exchanged for nails and cloth. In New Zealand, Cook had had trouble moderating the local people's desire for the mariners' things, their weapons especially. But he had no such trouble here. The problem he encountered in this place was the opposite: to try to create a market where none existed.

Day four is a midway point in the stopover at this place. Three full days had already passed, and four more were to follow before the *Endeavour* sailed out through the heads. It's probably fair to assume that by this time the captain had a fairly good idea about when he intended to set sail. He had made this stop mainly to replenish supplies, to carry out the work necessary for continuing his voyage along the east coast, to make some explorations of the country, and to rest his crew. It's possible he was not planning to stop many more times, or for very long again as he made his way northwards.

As it turned out, a series of landings were made as the ship sailed northwards along what is now the Queensland coast. Late May and early June were punctuated by fruitless searches for fresh water. The first stop was at a place Cook called Bustard Bay after the birds, about two-and-a-half weeks after leaving Botany Bay. The stopover was a short one, no more than two nights. Most of the time was spent looking for food and making short excursions in the country. No local people were seen, only their hearths.

At intervals from then on, some sailors would row ashore hopeful and row back disappointed. For instance, less than a week after Bustard Bay, Cook and another man landed at a place where they hoped the ship would spend a few days to wait for a better moon. Cook called this place Thirsty Sound because no water was found there. Rather than wait for the moon, they soon set sail. A week later, Zachary Hicks, Joseph Banks and Daniel Solander were sent ashore but 'met with nothing worth observing'. A couple of days passed before Cook, Banks and Solander rowed ashore and found little to satisfy. Once again Cook decided to press on rather than spend a night in the place.

The next time the ship stopped was unscheduled. While navigating the shoals on the far north coast, the *Endeavour* became stuck on the reef. First the ship had to be freed from the snag by throwing anchors, ballast and sundries overboard to lighten her load, all the while pumping like fury to release the water that was seeping into her holds through the holes made by the sharp-edged coral. Then the gashes were stuffed with oakum applied to the bottom of the ship with the aid of a sail, a technique that sailors call fothering. This done, the expedition was forced to stop for six weeks to carry out essential repairs at the place now known as Endeavour River. During this time, closer contact was made with the local people than had happened at Botany Bay. Had the wreck not occurred and the delay for repairs not been required, it is very likely that Botany Bay would have been the only place where Cook and company had an opportunity to form a connection with the local people.

However, at Botany Bay on day four Cook did not know what the future held. As far as he knew, the short stay in this sheltered bay might turn out to be the only opportunity he had to acquaint himself with the local inhabitants along the east coast of New Holland. As things stood on day four, not a lot of progress was being made on that score. Time was ticking by and still the knowledge that Cook and his companions had gained about the local people was sketchy at best. The locals had proved frustratingly elusive and it is tempting to think that the captain might have been regretting his recourse to the gun during his first face-to-face encounter with them on day one.

As is well known, Cook had sailed with secret instructions concerning what he was to do if he managed to locate *Terra Australis Incognita*. Those instructions directed him to 'cultivate a friendship and alliance' with the local inhabitants and to 'observe [their] Genius, Temper, Disposition and Number'. This place (he well knew) was not part of *that* mystery continent, just the uncharted east side of the already known landmass dubbed New Holland. The secret instructions served as a guide to him, nonetheless. In seeking out the local people, Cook was hoping to fill in some boxes for his superiors in England, but his motivations extend beyond simply wishing to please them. He was doing it for his own satisfaction as well. His curiosity compelled him to jump repeatedly from his boat when he saw local people on the shore. During the first voyage, an incipient ethnographic sensibility had already come into play. Between writing what Nicholas Thomas refers to as his 'first essay in anthropology' on the Haush people of Tierra del Fuego in January 1769 and this stopover in the territory of the Gweagal people on the east coast of New Holland nearly eighteen months later, Cook had honed his rudimentary skills in the observation of people different from himself and had amassed experience in encounters with them. But this is not to say that he had become an exemplary ethnographer, or that an insatiable interest in different people was what motivated him most.

He was not always adept at making contact with the local people he came across, as the experience at Botany Bay bears out. Even after his extensive experience over the previous year-and-a-half as he voyaged around the Pacific and spent extended time in New Zealand, Cook was clumsy in his attempts to open up an intercourse with the indigenous people at his first landing place on the east coast of New Holland. Nevertheless, regardless of his opening gambit a few days earlier, and the reaction of the local people to it, Cook remained steadfast in his hope that a connection would eventually be made with them.

After leaving better things at the local people's 'huts' in the morning, Cook, Solander, Banks and a party of men – with ten muskets between them, Banks tells us – hiked inland. One wonders if the objects had been left as payment-in-kind for the birds and animals that they would kill and the plants they would collect that day, or as some kind of insurance for safe passage through the local people's territory. The party walked all day 'till we compleatly tird ourselves, which was in the evening' according to Banks, or until three or four in the afternoon according to Cook. The entire day they saw only one local 'who ran from us as soon as he saw us', writes Banks. Cook tells us that 'at our first seting out one of them was seen the others I suppose had fled upon our approach'. By now, Cook seems to have been almost resigned to the fact that the local people would keep their distance. He expected them to flee. With their persistent absence, he would be forced to base his observations about their way of life on the traces he found scattered on the landscape.

On this excursion into the country the scant evidence he had to draw upon included only 'some hutts and places where the natives had been' and

> some trees that had been cut down by the natives with some sort of a blunt instrument and several trees that were barked the bark of which had been cut by the same Instrument, in many of the trees, especially the palms, were cut steps about 3 or 4 feet asunder for the conveniency of climeing them.

To this evidence of human habitation, Banks added that 'we saw many Indian houses and places where they had slept upon the grass without the least shelter'. As a calling card, they left more beads and ribbons behind.

Piecing together a picture of a people from the detritus of their daily life misses a lot. Observation obviously is no substitute for conversation when it comes to understanding other people. The mute landscape and the silent things could not provide a window onto beliefs, or religious practices, or social organisation, or attitudes to worlds seen and unseen. The voyagers did not learn, for instance, about the ways in which the local people tended the land. The cursory accounts that both James Cook and Joseph Banks give of the country they rambled across for a few hours are suggestive of just how intensely the local people managed this landscape, even though they do not ascribe the qualities of the place to the local people. The strangers were searching for sure signs of farming but were not adept at reading the landscape for evidence of firestick farming. Cook found the country

> deversified with woods, Lawns and Marshes; the woods are free from under wood of every kind and the trees are at such a distance from one a nother that the whole Country or at least a great part of it might be cultivated without being oblig'd to cut down a single tree.

Banks says that 'every place was coverd with vast quantities of grass'.

Much later on, when Australian historians turned their attention to Cook's short time at Botany Bay as part of the story of the nation, they scrutinised his assessment of the country's potential for agriculture and settlement. For them, Cook was a reconnaissance man, who laid the groundwork for white settlement. Missing from these mainly twentieth-century historical accounts is Cook's pursuit of the local people. They do not present him as a man equally interested in the people as he is in the place. They present the situation as though the local people had been summarily dealt with on the first day, and for the remainder of the time Cook and his company had the place all to themselves. This is the structure of the narrative that can be found in G. A. Wood's *The Discovery of Australia* and repeated in the first volume of Manning Clark's monumental *A History of Australia*. A paragraph or two is devoted to describing the episode of the first landing, which is immediately followed by others that focus on Cook's and Banks' exploration and assessment of the country. These subsequent paragraphs are written without any reference at all to the local people. Indeed, these historians typically portray Cook and Banks as though they were exploring an unpeopled landscape. They present the landscape as though it was empty. Their accounts are strangely at odds with Cook's own.

While the overland party was out shooting birds, observing huts and marks cut in trees, testing the quality of the soil, leaving presents for the locals and catching a glimpse of something that looked like a rabbit, John Gore, the third lieutenant (after Cook and Hicks), was in the bay on a boat with some men 'drudging' for oysters, as his captain had instructed him to do. John Gore had experience. Like Robert Molyneux and a handful of others in the crew, Gore had sailed with Captain Samuel Wallis on the *Dolphin* between 1766 and 1768 on its second voyage to the Pacific. Unlike them, he had earlier sailed on the *Dolphin* with Commodore John Byron from 1764 to 1766 on its first voyage. By the time he got to the east coast of New Holland, John Gore had almost completed his third voyage around the world. And when Captain Cook was killed in Hawai'i in 1779, it was the veteran John Gore who took command and safely shepherded the ships back to England.

I first made acquaintance with John Gore in *An Account of the Discovery of Tahiti from the Journal of George Robertson, Master of H. M. S. Dolphin*. In its opening pages it describes an incident at Tahiti in June 1767, when it had been Gore's job to take out the cutter to sound the bay in preparation for the ship's anchorage, and Robertson describes the situation in evocative detail. While out sounding, Gore and his men had been surrounded by increasing numbers of local people in large canoes. The situation became heated and confused, leading to stone-throwing in one direction and shooting in return. It was an especially fraught episode, one which makes Robert Molyneux' experience of sounding the entrance to this bay a few days before look a little tame. As I read more widely about Gore, I found numerous vignettes in the records from each of the voyages he had been on that describe him in his dealings with the local people he encountered. He was a man who had had his fair share of humiliations and frustrations at the hands of the local people he met, but there are also many indications of his humanity in his interactions on the beaches he crossed. There is a portrait of him in the collections of the National Library of Australia in Canberra, which shows a gentle face seemingly lacking in guile (Plate 17). He seems only to have kept a journal on this voyage until the end of 1769, or else the later volume covering 1770 has been lost. In the volumes that do survive, he heads his pages with the title 'Remarkable Observations and Accidents'. He is a man willing to acknowledge, appreciate even, the accidental and the contingent.

In the hierarchy of the *Endeavour*'s company, John Gore was a rank below Zachary Hicks and a rank above Robert Molyneux. Molyneux and Hicks had had their close encounters with the local people – Molyneux on day one and Hicks on day two. Today it was Gore's turn.

While he was 'up the bay' in the boat dredging for oysters, John Gore believed that he had been invited by signs to come ashore by some of the locals. He declined the imputed invitation, prudently in Cook's view. It's uncertain whether such an invitation had been offered. The strangers had not yet learnt the signs for 'come' and for 'go' in this place.

When he had finished dredging for oysters, he decided he would send the boat back to the ship and walk back to the watering place along the beach in company with a midshipman. There were three midshipmen listed in the ship's company: John Bootie, Jonathon Monkhouse and Patrick Saunders. Which of them made the excursion on this occasion? The records don't say. John Bootie kept a log, but he doesn't mention this incident in it so perhaps he was not the one.

As Gore and his companion ambled along the beach they were, according to Banks, 'overtaken by 22 Indians who followed him often within 20 yards, parleying but never daring to attack him tho they were all armd with lances'. Cook tells us that 'whenever Mr Gore made a stand

and fac'd them they stood also and notwithstanding they were all arm'd they never offerd to attack him'. Their trek had turned into a tango. (Once again, Banks and Cook were not eyewitnesses to this episode. They were somewhere else, far away from where the action was. They report the testimony of participants.)

The scene has something in common with the incident involving Lieutenant Hicks a couple of days before. The group kept their distance but repeatedly made a stand. On no occasion did they attack. They were all the time talking, perhaps shouting, maybe cajoling. Parleying is how Banks describes it. What were the locals saying as they parleyed? Perhaps inquiring where the strangers were from? Asking them their business? Insisting that they leave? They were ushering them out again, and perhaps trying to ensure that they stayed on the littoral margin rather than straying too far inland.

Details about what happened next are a bit sketchy in the accounts provided by James Cook and Joseph Banks in their journals. The sketchiness underscores the confusion of the situation. The shaky, clumsy bits in the written records often 'attest to what was hard to understand or hard to admit', writes Nicholas Thomas. This much is certain. After their walk, turn and face, walk, turn and face, walk, turn and face along the beach, Gore and his man finally reached the group of mariners who were gathered at the watering place. This included the usual party of waterers and some others, perhaps men who had earlier been on the excursion into the country led by Cook and others. They had made it safely to their destination, unharmed but a little rattled.

Probably as soon as they made it to the watering place, Gore and his man told the gathering there what had happened to them. Perhaps they demonstrated the various movements. Perhaps they conjectured about what it all meant. The experience would have swiftly become a story. All the while, the twenty-two local men remained at a distance – about half a mile, according to Banks' report. Once again, the two separate groups stood huddled at a distance from each other on the shore, each intensely aware of the other. They had been in this situation before.

Just then, three or four of the mariners who had heard Gore's story (or who had perhaps witnessed what happened to him) decided to approach the group of local men still standing half a mile away. Joseph Banks describes this little party as 'more curious perhaps than prudent'.

The only one identified by name in the records is the ship's surgeon, Dr William Brougham Monkhouse. (This Monkhouse was the cousin, some say the uncle, of the Monkhouse who was a midshipman.) I got to know a little about Dr Monkhouse by reading his account of the expedition's first landfall in New Zealand at Poverty Bay (now Gisborne), about six months before the *Endeavour* arrived at Botany Bay. In it, he describes a situation in which some local Maori men were keen to get their hands on the voyagers' things. 'Their eyes and hands [were] as quick as those of the most accomplished pickpocket', he wrote. But he was willing to play along with them. He explains:

> I happened to be the most forward of our company, and was engaged with three of these young active heroes at one time: this new manoeuvre disconcerted me for a moment, but my situation presently taught me to play the counterpart in these curious gesticulations.

He could act the part in these impromptu cross-cultural performances.

His account of the *Endeavour*'s time in New Zealand is the only surviving fragment of a larger journal that he kept on the voyage. If the pages of it covering the time at Botany Bay were found, the story that follows would be more elaborate than what can be pieced together from Cook and Banks. Monkhouse has an eye for small details, a surgeon's precision in his explications, and clearly enjoys making himself the centre of his narrative. There is a portrait of him in the collections of the National Library in Canberra (Plate 18). Looking sideways out of the frame, he strikes me as mischievous – cheeky Monkhouse? – but my judgment is infused with my knowledge of what happened in New Zealand and what is about to happen at Botany Bay.

'When they came pretty near [the locals]', writes Banks, 'they pretended to be afraid and ran from them'. Cook describes Monkhouse and the others as 'making a sham retreat'. This is a game, an act, a performance, a display. They are mimicking the local men, playing back to them their own behaviour but in an exaggerated way. There is a fine line between mimicry and mockery, and it's especially thin in this episode. How much were they hamming it up? Did they scream and squeal when they pretended to be afraid? Did they exaggerate their urgency to flee? At this point, Monkhouse's missing journal is acutely missed. What was in their minds when they played their parts? Whose idea was it? Was it a plan hatched as they walked towards the men standing in the distance, or had they been waiting for the opportunity for some time? Had they rehearsed it before? Were they motivated by a desire to make contact, or to ease their boredom?

Mimicry was a device used quite commonly by one or more sides in cross-cultural encounters as a means for making contact, and its repeated appearance in voyager and explorer accounts has led many scholars to ruminate about its purposes, its uses and its effects. There are celebrated incidents in the annals of early contact history in Australia when relations were warmed by mimetic performances. The navigator and explorer Matthew Flinders, for instance, appears to have been especially attuned to its potential. Before leaving King Georges Sound in 1801 after a short stay there, he directed the marines in his expedition to practise their drill on shore for the pleasure of the local people. Flinders had already observed the resemblances between his men's uniforms and the body paint that the local people sometimes used. His intuition about ceremonial behaviour and its appeal to the local people proved correct. It was not long before an old local man was imitating the soldiers, marching in time with them and mimicking their gestures.

In this incident, separated by many decades and many miles from the one at Botany Bay in 1770, the performance and the mimicry serve to highlight resemblances rather than differences between the two groups. It becomes a conduit for recognition. But the impetus behind Monkhouse's mimicry does not seem so benign. It's hard not to see something more sinister behind it, and to interpret it as less an attempt to *make contact* and more as an expression of the *distance* that the strangers perceived between themselves and the locals. Only cowards flee, they seemed to be saying by means of their sham retreat. The mimicry of retreat (out of all possible behaviour to imitate) registered the low opinion that some in the crew were slowly forming about the local people. They mimicked an action that the voyagers did not admire, and they could afford to play the clown because they did not fear the object of their ridicule.

Yet, at the same time, the very thing that the voyagers did not understand, or that went against their own way of doing things, was 'displaced into the context of mimicry'. By mimicking the unfamiliar and unsettling action of retreat that the local men had used repeatedly, the voyager role-players in this vignette were reflecting (consciously or otherwise) on what they had observed of the local men. Through their play-acting they tested the limits of the local people's authority in a mode that was less risky than direct challenge. It was a safer option. And in this respect, their game produced results.

This mimicry, this mockery, this provocation, this play-acting – however one might want to interpret it – immediately incited four of the local men to throw their spears at the men who had imitated them. The spears did not strike any of them, but landed beyond them. They had been thrown about forty yards, so Banks reckoned. Monkhouse and his men stopped and 'began to collect the lances, on which the Indians slowly retired', Banks tells us. Had they collected them as trophies, or as *aides de memoire* for when they recounted the story in later times? These were spears-as-souvenirs. Maybe one of these spears was among those that ended up in the *wunderkammer* in the library at Cambridge.

This was only the *second* time in four days that the locals had thrown their spears at the strangers. The other time was during the first landing, when two or three spears had been thrown at the landing party after it got ashore. They discharged them only after provocation, or in response to a show of force from the strangers. On both occasions the locals shot their weapons near, but beyond, their targets, which suggests that the skill was more in missing than in meeting their man. This suggestion gains substance with consideration of like incidents in the early years of British settlement. One that comes to mind is the spearing of Governor Phillip at Manly in September 1790, and particularly its closing scene. It was a complex incident. Phillip was wounded in the shoulder by a spear thrown determinedly by one man from among a very large group. It was as though the action had been planned, and was endorsed by those the spear-thrower was in company with. Immediately, Phillip's small party of men fled with him along the sand and into their boat. All the while, other local men threw spears at them, none of which hit.

Commenting on this state of affairs, the historian Inga Clendinnen says that in her mind this is 'clear evidence the spears were not thrown with the intent to injure'. If they had been designed to wound, then the local men would have had little trouble in lodging their lances in the moving targets. From the outset of British colonisation in 1788, the local people all around the settlement had been admired for their accuracy with their weapons and hunting implements across distances greater than the one between the congregation on the beach and the retreating colonists that day. The shower of spears landing *about* but not *in* the retreating party was probably designed to remind the British of the potential force the local people possessed. This was a display of their authority, but not the enactment or actualisation of it. Indeed, Clendinnen suggests that even Governor Phillip ought not to have been wounded that day, if only he had known to duck from what was likely a ritual spearing. As at Manly in 1790, the local men at Botany Bay in 1770 had once more displayed their authority but had not yet thought it either necessary or wise to inflict a wound upon any of those strangers in their midst.

Immediately after the spears had been thrown, Cook, Solander and Tupaia, who had just arrived at the watering place from their excursion in the 'woods', made their way towards the local men, but by this time they were already making their departure. Cook, Solander and Tupaia continued following them while all others stayed behind, including Banks. 'This however', according to Banks, 'did not stop the Indians who walkd leasurely away till our people were tird of following them'. Cook explains that 'Dr Solander, I, and Tupia made all the haste we could after them but could by neither words nor actions prevail upon them to come near us'. The locals had once more got away from Cook.

So ended day four.

The FIFTH DAY

The morning of day five was windy and rainy after heavy downpours and thunder and lightning overnight. This stopped Cook 'from makeing an excursion up to the head of the bay as I intended'. Banks was pleased for the respite the rain brought because he and Solander 'who had got already so many plants were well contented to find an excuse for staying on board to examine them a little at least'. And so their morning was spent on board the ship. The crew also went to work on the ship, 'scrubbing and cleaning the ship's bottom and giving her a good cleaning within board', according to the log compiled by Wilkinson, the master's mate. By mid-morning the weather cleared. The wooders and the waterers returned to the shore, the former delivering a longboat full of timber to the ship by the end of the day and the latter being able to complete the watering of the ship to '80 tons'.

In the afternoon, Cook, Banks, Solander and Tupaia made 'a little excursion along the Sea Coast to the southward', Cook tells us. Banks says:

> we returnd to our old occupation of collecting, in which we had our usual good success. Tupia who strayed from us in pursuit of Parrots, of which he shot several, told us on his return that he had seen nine Indians who ran from him as soon as they perceived him.

Likewise, Cook noted:

> at our first entering the woods we saw 3 of the natives who made off as soon as they saw us; more of them were seen by others of our people who likewise made off as soon as they found they were discovered.

They were avoiding him, again.

Throughout the five days that the mariners had been in the bay, the locals had on numerous occasions fled when the strangers suddenly appeared, or when they approached them from the sea. This habit was not new. As Sylvia Hallam notes more generally,

> many were the occasions on which Aboriginal Australians simply kept out of the way in order to avoid an encounter with men they did not know, where there were no correct forms to follow.

Fleeting glimpses of fleeing people provide evidence for the exercise in evasion that the locals used as a strategem for dealing with strangers.

Yet there was a change. Up until day five, avoidance had been used in combination with advance. From this day on, organised advance by groups of men was dropped. The local men stopped approaching in formation the sailors on the shore. They did not follow them at a distance along the shore, or parley with them. Over the first four days there was certainly no great progress made towards the establishment of close relations. Nevertheless, in the opening days the local men had at least seemed prepared to try to communicate their wishes to the strangers, using a set of both practised and opportunistic responses. On day five and in the days that followed, they stopped doing even this and began to 'avoid encounters altogether'. This was one option short of the least favourable, which would have involved entering into hostilities with them.

Visible presence became obvious absence. Whether this was a direct outcome of the incident the evening before involving Dr Monkhouse and his men, is impossible to tell. Perhaps it is a coincidence, but it could have been a consequence. I am inclined to think the latter. Dr Monkhouse and his unnamed companions, it seems, were responsible for one of those actions that change in noticeable and perhaps irredeemable ways the cadence of a contact experience.

It has been common for Australian historians to portray the encounter in broad brushstrokes, in which the response of the local people is painted in monotone. They are portrayed as inflexible – 'sullenly hostile', according to the Australian historian G. A. Wood. It is as though all their actions were derived from their pre-existing nature, already fixed and inflexible, rather than varied and responsive as the situation demanded. The Monkhouse incident and its aftermath destabilises this perception. There is a noticeable change in the behaviour of the local people, but it can only be detected when the encounter is reconstructed as a series of action-sequences one after the other, rather than portrayed as an amorphous event in which the days, hours, mornings or evenings are not distinguished one from the other. A close reading of the voyager journals indicates a shift in tempo, temperament and temperature on day five, and it was not simply because of the weather. Something had happened to change the local people's responses and reactions to the strangers. With an alteration in strategy, things quietened down.

So ended day five.

The SIXTH DAY

*T*he weather was clear – 'moderate and fine', according to most of the logs. In the morning, Cook and some men went in the 'pinnace to the head of the bay accompan'd by Drs Soland[er] and Munkhouse in order to examine the Country and to try to form some connections with the natives'. 'To try to form some connections with the natives': this is the first time in Cook's journal entries covering the days at Botany Bay that this intention is made explicit. It won't be the last.

Cook had consistently hoped to fall in with the local people as he made his excursions around the bay and into the country over the previous days. He had left things for them, which he had hoped would be a conduit to contact. He had approached them when he saw them. He had more than once followed them for a distance into the country. He had taken whatever opportunities had presented themselves in the course of his daily activities. But now on day six he was on a mission. He could wait no longer for an encounter to emerge as though organically. He was going to try to make a meeting happen. With only a day or two left by his reckoning before it was time to sail from this place, this particular project had become more urgent. He redoubled his efforts.

No matter that Cook had become more single-minded in this pursuit, the experience of the previous days was simply repeated. On the morning's

85

excursion to the head of the bay with Doctors Monkhouse and Solander, they met with

> 10 or 12 of [the local people] fishing each in a small Canoe who retired in to shoald water upon our approach, others again we saw at the first place we landed at who took to their Canoes and fled before we came near them.

The local people were out and about, but they remained steadfastly uninterested in meeting with the strangers.

That on this occasion Cook was as interested in forming a connection with the locals as he was in examining the country is well reflected in his journal account. He explains that his party went next 'to the head of the inlet where we landed and travel'd some distance inland'. For a few sentences Cook describes the country. He observes that the country is

> much the same as I have before described but the land much richer, for in stead of sand I found in many places a deep black Soil which we thought was capable of produceing any kind of grain, at present it produceth besides timber as fine meadow as ever was seen.

'Capable of produceing any kind of grain': this was a line that appealed to the would-be colonists who read Cook's reports. 'As fine meadow as ever was seen' was another one that confused Captain Phillip, in charge of the first fleet. He could not find this fine meadow, or any other, when he arrived at the place with his cargo of convicts in 1788. That this was a very variable landscape is again confirmed by Cook when he writes:

> However we found it not all like this, some few places were very rocky but this I believe to be uncommon; the stone is sandy and very proper for building &ca.

He did not realise that some of the variability was managed. However, he added to his account a little more hope to future colonists, who would have at their disposal materials for making mansions.

While some early (and not so early) twentieth-century Australian historians have spotlighted these sentences as signs to settlement, they have largely ignored Cook's other special interest on this excursion on day six. 'After we had sufficiently examined this part', he then writes, 'we return'd to the boat and seeing some smook and Canoes at a nother part we went theither in the hopes of meeting with the people'. James Cook was nothing if not persistent. He had not yet been completely cowed by the local people's tendency to leave as he approached. 'But they made off as we approached'. His advances were met with the same response every time. All he could do was describe what they left behind. On this occasion he went one step further and tasted their mussels roasting on the fire, which he paid for with beads.

The response of Joseph Banks to the persistent elusiveness of the local people was different from that of James Cook. Banks gave up chasing them and devoted himself instead to his 'immensely large' collection of plant specimens. On the sixth day, he spent his entire time drying his specimens in the open air. He was helped in this task by the fact that the ship's sails had been 'loosened' and laid out to dry after a night of heavy rain. Banks spread near 200 quires of drying paper on a sail spread out in the sun, turning them from time to time. Each quire would consist of about 25 sheets. That's a lot of specimens sunning on a sail on the shore. 'By this means', Banks writes, 'they came on board at night in very good condition'.

If Banks was grumpily ignoring the local people, they were not completely ignoring him. While he went about his business that day, close by were eleven men in eleven canoes. They were 'striking fish', writes Banks, and 'they came within about ½ mile of us intent on their own employments and not at all regarding us'. This is a study in mutual disregard. Disregard demands discipline. Despite himself, Joseph Banks seemed to have stumbled across the most felicitous approach to take towards the locals in this bay. Ignore them and they might venture to come close.

This is what seems to have happened when the expedition was held up at Endeavour River for those six weeks in July and August 1770 making emergency repairs to the ship after it had been snagged on the coral. With all their attention given to making the vessel seaworthy again, the captain and the crew largely ignored the locals. Three weeks passed before any interaction occurred. And when it did, it was instigated by the local people *approaching* rather than Cook *pursuing*. When one morning some local people finally ventured close to the ship, Cook held firm to his new-found method of pretending to pay them no attention. He writes in his journal:

> some [of his crew] were for going over in a boat to them but this I would not suffer but let them alone without seeming to take any notice of them.

He had learnt the technique from his experience with the locals at Botany Bay, it seems.

This diffident strategy paid dividends. 'At length', he writes,

> two came in the Canoe so near the ship as to take some things we throw'd them, after this they went away and brought over the other two and came again along side nearer then they had done before and took such trifles as we gave them.

Contact had been made slowly and cautiously. In this context, it seems, the gifts offered were accepted. Imagine what might have happened had Cook used this method at Botany Bay.

Back at Botany Bay, while Joseph Banks tended to his plants all day, Tupaia appears to have occupied himself by drawing what he saw. One of the treasures from the expedition's time at Botany Bay is a drawing he made of three local people fishing from two canoes (Plate 19). The two figures in the front canoe manoeuvre their vessel with short paddles. Their arms are extended the exact same distance, the right one forward, the left one back, which suggests that they are paddling along. The figure who sits in the bow of the canoe appears to gaze ahead, but the one in the stern looks to steal a glimpse of the artist drawing him. The third figure is in a canoe behind them. He stands in his vessel, bent forwards, taking concentrated aim with his gig at a fish in the water. The spear the man trains on the big-eyed fish has four neatly drawn, dead straight prongs.

Tupaia is careful and precise not only with the details of the local people's things but also with their physical features, including the colour of their skin, the style of their hair and the shapes and postures of their bodies. He has rendered the three figures in an inky black, quite distinct from the brown he uses in his picture of Javanese drummers, or the pink applied for the skin of a Tahitian dancing girl. He has gone to some trouble to illustrate their hair with a series of short black strokes. Tupaia's portrayal of the New Hollanders' hair concords with Banks' later written description: 'their hair ... they wore croppd close round their ears'.

The two figures in the front canoe seem a little thinner, and effeminate even, in their body shape and posture compared with the figure in the back canoe. This suggests to me that they may be women or perhaps young or adolescent boys. It is impossible to tell for sure, because he does not show their naked fronts. The figure in the back canoe is, however, definitely a man. The penis that Tupaia has drawn on him makes that clear. Not even Parkinson seemed prepared to be quite so explicit in his drawings of the local people. In his drawing of one of the two armed local men he has carefully placed the shield he holds to obscure his genitals. Paradoxically, the fact that Tupaia does not show the fronts of the bodies of the two figures in the first canoe – obscuring their chests or breasts – may be used to support an argument that they are indeed women. That they do not hold spears may be further evidence because, as the archaeologist Val Attenbrow notes: 'It was well-documented that in 1788 fishing with hook and line was the specific task of women'. These figures do not obviously hold a fishing line, but neither do they hold spears. For what it's worth, in my opinion Tupaia has drawn a scene of a man out fishing with his two wives. Judging by the subjects of some of his other drawings made during this voyage, he seems to have been interested in relations between people. He has drawn a scene: a domestic scene, rather than a series of separate figures in the way that Parkinson has done in his preliminary drawings.

Tupaia's drawing has long been preserved in the collections of the British Library but it took some time before it, along with a collection of other drawings in the same style, was confidently ascribed to him. Before this, their creator was typically described in the literature as the 'Artist of the Chief Mourner' because that was the subject of one of the more striking images in the series. The theory that Joseph Banks was the artist circulated for some time, but in the end the evidence for the drawings' origins came from the discovery of a letter that was written by Joseph Banks, part of which reads:

> Tupaia the Indian who came with me from Otaheite Learned to draw in a way not Quite unintelligible. The genius for Caricature which all wild people possess Led him to Caricature me & he drew me with a nail in my hand delivering to an Indian who sold me a Lobster.

The drawing of the exchange of a lobster for a nail belongs to the same series as the one of the three figures in the two canoes. From his off-handed reference to 'wild' people in the letter, one is tempted to say that Banks is perfectly capable of representing himself as a caricature without the aid of Tupaia's artistic ability.

Tupaia had begun to learn to draw figures on paper in Tahiti when he made friends with the voyage artist Sydney Parkinson, but was probably already 'skilled in painting and dyeing bark-cloth', according to the New Zealand historian Anne Salmond. He had apparently been 'enthralled with Sydney Parkinson's sketches and paintings', and indeed Tupaia's pictures have some of the same humane quality that characterises Parkinson's pictures of people. As Bernard Smith says: 'it was Parkinson who developed not only the most sympathetic relationships with but also the greatest sympathy for the peoples of the Pacific', a quality which Smith ascribes at least in part to Parkinson's Quaker upbringing.

There is certainly something of that sympathy at play even in the couple of quick sketches that Parkinson made showing local men in canoes. One of these appears in the top right-hand corner on the page of rough drawings already mentioned (Plate 4). He's easy to miss, overshadowed by the two larger figures at the bottom of the page. Even though the sketch is minuscule, Parkinson has been able to capture some personality in the man's visage and to convey something of the strength of his body. He's a recognisable figure.

While Banks was tending his plants and an estimated eleven locals were fishing from canoes nearby and Tupaia was making his drawing of some of them, 'several of our people were shooting' on the shore, explains Banks. 'One Indian may be prompted by curiosity landed', he elaborates,

> hauld up his canoe and went towards them; he stayed about a quarter of an hour and then launchd his boat and went off, probably that time had been spent in watching behind trees to see what our people did.

Peppered throughout the large archive of early colonial explorations in Australia are many, many references to the sense that some explorers had of being watched from behind trees. As the consistently perceptive Bishop Salvado of the Benedictine Order, who arrived in the colony of Western Australia in 1846, wrote: 'Europeans travelling in the bush often fail to see a single native, whereas there are a number of them hidden behind trees watching their every movement'. Only when the activities of the men from the *Endeavour* had slowed down at Botany Bay to the pace that it takes for plants to dry, did they become aware of how much they were being *observed*. They were not the only observant ones in this place.

Once he had completed caring for his collection, Banks made a small excursion into the woods 'in order to shoot any thing I could meet with and found a large quantity of Quails'. He was not after food, but more specimens and he was, he explains, killing for variety not volume.

When Cook returned to the ship in the evening, he must have asked his men for their observations of the local people that day. He had had no luck himself but was interested if any of his company had. He was told that 'none of the natives had appear'd near the watering place'. This was unusual. However, he was further informed that 'about 20 of them had been fishing in their canoes at no great distance from us'. These were probably the ones whom Banks had described. Perhaps this gave Cook heart that there was still a possibility of forming a connection with them, although his experience of the day must have made him feel that the prospect of a meeting was slight. Time was running out. At the end of day six, the object of opening up an intercourse with the local people remained unfulfilled.

It is worth noting the shift in emphasis in the concerns covered by James Cook and Joseph Banks in their respective journals. Cook's section on the eight days at Botany Bay had begun with only passing reference to the local people because his attention was squarely on getting the ship to anchor, getting his men to work and getting his bearings in the bay. Once that had been done, his attention turned towards the local people and their country. Joseph Banks' journal entries follow a different curve. He is detailed in his descriptions about the local people in the opening days, but as they remain elusive his patience with them falters. His comments about them in the closing days of the eight-day encounter are either dismissively brief or non-existent. He has much more to say about his plants than about the people.

Cook had brought back from his excursion fruit from trees, which Banks described as 'much in colour and shape resembling cherries'. The company ate them 'with much pleasure tho they had little to recommend them but a light acid', said Banks. Another meal of local foodstuffs brought the day to a close.

So ended day six.

The SEVENTH DAY

Cook had planned to sail this morning but was prevented from doing so. 'In the AM . . . the wind would not permit us to sail', he wrote at the start of his entry for day seven. This helps to explain in part his behaviour of the day before. If he had sailed this morning, then day six would have been his very last opportunity to form *a connection* with the locals. However, with departure delayed for another day, he had a new day at his disposal to try again. And try again he did.

As the wind would not allow them to sail, 'I sent out some parties into the Country to try to form some Connections with the natives', he explains. 'To try to form some connections with the natives' – he has made this intention explicit again. No more looking around the landscape. No more charting the coastline. All other jobs were complete or almost complete. The ship was wooded and watered and the supplies replenished and stocked. There were only two tasks left to do. One was to leave a record of the ship's stay in this place, a declaration that the *Endeavour* was here, which the wooders did on shore in the morning. The anonymous author of one of the journals noted in his distinctive hand: 'Mark'd a Tree in his Britanick Majestys Name with the Name of the Ship, Month & Year'. The other incomplete project was not quite so easy to realise. To make contact with the locals was now the main aim. Cook increased the number of men devoted to this task by sending out some parties, not just one but, no matter what manpower was thrown at it, this proved to be the hardest task of all.

Joseph Banks did not join these parties scouting for the local people. His interest lay elsewhere. His journal for day seven begins: 'Myself in the woods botanising as usual, now quite void of fear as our neighbours have turnd out such rank cowards'. An indictment indeed. He had given up on them altogether.

Even with parties of men spreading out across the landscape, there was not much to report in the way of cross-cultural meetings. One encounter was slightly farcical and more incidental than intentional. 'One of our midshipmen', reports Banks,

> stragling by himself a long way from any one else met by accident with a very old man and woman and some children: they were setting under a tree and neither party saw the other till they were close together.

It's a touching scene that Banks paints of this incident.

> They shewd signs of fear but did not attempt to run away. He had nothing about him to give them but some Parrots which he had shot: these they refused, withdrawing themselves from his hand when he offerd them in token either of extreme fear or disgust.

The locals were still refusing the gifts the strangers thrust in their direction. Nothing they had to offer, even familiar fare, would entice them to come closer. The officer was cautious in his dealings with this group of young and old.

> He stayd however with them but a very short time, for seing many canoes fishing at a small distance he feard that the people in them might observe him and come ashore to the assistance of the old people, who in all probability belongd to them.

Some vestiges of fear among the crew about what the local people might be capable of in defence of their kin remained.

As on the day before, the locals continued to fish from their canoes near the strangers, although they tended to fish in quite large groups compared with the numbers seen engaged in this activity during the first few days. On the first day four were seen together, two days ago twelve, yesterday about twenty. Today, Banks tells us, seventeen canoes were seen 'fishing near our people in the same manner as yesterday only stayed rather longer', and then offers by way of explanation, 'emboldend a little I suppose by having yesterday met with no kind of molestation'. Perhaps this was leading somewhere. Eventually, had time allowed, the distance might have been bridged.

In the afternoon, Banks went ashore on the north-west side of the bay. He described the country a good way away from the shore as like 'our Moors in England, as no trees grow upon it but every thing is coverd with a thin brush of plants about as high as the knees'. These moors were later given the name Banksmeadow. While Banks was about his business in the country collecting what he could find, others were along the shore snaring fish and striking rays. There would be fish for supper again that night; it was business as usual.

Dr William Monkhouse was hanging around the shore again, this time in company with one other. Cook says he was 'in the woods not far from the watering place'. Banks places him 'a long way from the people [i.e. the waterers] and coming out of a thicket'. The details are a little contradictory. This is another one of those confusing incidents, the confusion of which is registered in the written accounts of it, which perhaps derive from different sources or from varying degrees of elaboration as the story is told and retold. Either way, whether close by the watering place or far away from it, Dr Monkhouse was discovered by some local men, who appear to have been on the lookout for him as he was on the lookout for some of them.

Joseph Banks reports that a group were 'standing about 50 yards from' Monkhouse when he first observed them. Cook says that they 'at first seemd to wait his coming'. Monkhouse had not accidentally stumbled across them; they had stationed themselves in his path, or so it seems. 'One of these', Banks tells us, 'gave a signal by a word pronounced loud, on which a lance was thrown out of the wood at [Monkhouse] which however came not very near him'. They were decoys. 'As he was going up to them', Cook tells us, he 'had a dart thrown at him out of a tree which narrowly escaped him'. The locals had ambushed the doctor. This was no random assault. They had marked their man. Three days after the surgeon had played his little game with the locals and had made his 'sham retreat', they played a little game with him. The game he had started was still going.

On one detail, Cook and Banks agree. Once the spear had been thrown, the locals quickly departed the scene. 'As soon as the fellow had thrown the dart', writes Cook 'he descended the tree and made off and with him all the rest'. 'The 6 Indians', writes Banks, *on seeing that it had not taken effect ran away in an instant, but on turning about towards the place from whence the lance came [Monkhouse] saw a young lad, who undoubtedly had thrown it, come down from a tree where he had been Stationd probably for that purpose; he descended however and ran away so quick that it was impossible even to attempt to pursue him.*

This was consistent with their practice. Every time they threw a missile at the mariners, they walked away. None of the journals say so one way or another, but it wouldn't be surprising if Monkhouse souvenired this particular spear. I can imagine him using it as a prop when he recounted, to whomever would listen to the story, the time when it was thrown at him from a tree.

So ended day seven.

In the END

The EIGHTH DAY

With the wind continuing northerly, the morning of day eight provided no better prospects for sailing. Departure was postponed for another day. In light of this, Cook sent the yawl out again 'afishing', and went himself with 'a party of Men into the Country but met with nothing extraordinary'. In company with Daniel Solander, Joseph Banks 'employed the whole day in collecting specimens of as many things as we possibly could to be examined at sea'. There is something almost frenzied about Banks' and Solander's collecting as the day for leaving drew closer, like a last mad rush for souvenirs at the end of a holiday.

On this day, the last day, the mariners had the place completely to themselves. Banks notes in passing that 'no Indians were seen by any body during the whole day'. They did not come in their canoes to fish close by; they did not approach the strangers boldly in groups; they did not hide in trees waiting to surprise a passer-by. No words or things, no glances or lances, were exchanged that day. The local people did not appear at all. Perhaps they too had finished their business in this place. There was nothing left for them to do. They had tried variously to encourage the strangers to meet with them on proper (or at least tolerable) terms, or to leave post haste. Neither result had yet eventuated, and so perhaps they thought it best simply to stay away.

To be abandoned in this way was, one imagines, an unnerving end to the voyagers' stopover in this place. For some of the sailors, James Cook included, the situation might have reinforced a sense of failure in respect to making contact with the locals. There had been no meeting of any note between the two groups, and there was little or no prospect that one would take place now. For other mariners, Joseph Banks included, it was more likely to have confirmed the opinion they had formed that the locals were no better than 'rank cowards'. If there had been a contest at play in this place, by their absence the local people were crowned the losers by some of the crew.

To be there or not to be there is a choice. To not appear at all is as much a conscious and deliberate action as it is to approach boldly in formation or to shout loud and long from the shore. In this instance, the agreed course of action that they would stay away from the strangers came only after other options had been exhausted. Over the past week or so the locals had doggedly sought to deter, ignore and avoid the sailors, which Hallam argues are three distinct dispositions that can be combined into a repeating pattern in chance meetings with strangers. Deter, ignore, avoid: the locals had used them all, but none of them had worked with these interlopers. Best to leave and best to leave them alone, seems to have been the conclusion. In sequences used with strangers 'the final movement is retreat', says Hallam. The orchestrated dance with strangers in this place had at last, it seems, reached its final movement. The show was almost over.

With no local people present, and with little else to report, Cook's account of the activities during day eight is unsurprisingly short. He records that in the evening the yawl returned, 'having caught two Sting rays weighing near 600 pounds'. This was a repeat of the success of the previous day, when the yawl had come back to the ship with stingrays 'upwards of 4 hundred weight; one single one weighed 240 lb exclusive of the entrails'. The sailors were laying in supplies. The crew's time in the bay had begun with a feast of freshly caught fish. Now it ended with a last supper of freshly speared rays, although at least one of the logs says that 'it was very strong and made a number of eat of it sickly'.

The size of the stingrays snared on the last two days impressed the crew. All the journals record their weight. Banks says that the second lieutenant had again gone out 'striking and took several large Stingrays the biggest of which weighd without his gutts 236 pounds'. Herman Sporing, the third artist in Joseph Banks' retinue, produced a series of fine pencil drawings of stingrays caught in the bay, perhaps this celebrated one included (Plate 21).

In his journal, Sydney Parkinson explains that:

> The rays are of an enormous size: one of them which we caught weighed two hundred and thirty-nine pounds, and another three hundred and twenty-six. They tasted very much like the European rays, and the viscera had an agreeable flavour, not unlike stewed turtle. These rays, and shell-fish, are the natives chief food.

On the latter point Parkinson disagrees with Cook, who in his summary of Botany Bay claimed that: 'Sting rays I believe [the locals] do not eat because I never saw the least remains of one near any of their hutts or fire places'. Throughout his journal, Richard Pickersgill, the master's mate, insists on calling them stingerrays.

On the last day Cook gave some thought, but not much, to choosing a name for the bay. Stingrays were the only thing worth talking about on the eighth day, so that made the decision easy. He records the name and its rationale in his journal. 'The great quantity of these sort of fish found in this place occasioned my giving it the name of Sting ray's harbour', he writes. True to form, Pickersgill renders it Stingerray Bay. There are copies of various charts of the bay: Cook's original one along with some made later by men of the first fleet (Plate 20). Looking at them, I am surprised and more than a little delighted by the resemblance of Sting Ray's Harbour to the shape of a stingray. The bay's shoreline has that soft-edged diamond-shape of a ray's body. Had the local people drawn any association between the shape of the bay and the sea creature? The art curator Djon Mundine noticed the similarity when he recently described the bay as 'stingray in shape', but does not comment on the symbolism of the stingray, if any, to the local people.

Despite the neat fit between name and bay, Sting Ray's Harbour was a name that did not last long. Probably by August or September 1770 – that is, four or so months after the expedition had been there – the name Sting Ray's Harbour had been overridden and overwritten by the name Botany Bay. The large number of plants collected by Joseph Banks and Daniel Solander, the import of which became more and more apparent as the ship progressed northward, were honoured by the new name (Plate 22). 'It is not surprising', muses Nicholas Thomas, 'that the science [the name] commemorated dealt with plants rather than people. What name could have expressed the failure of communication that took place here?' The failure of one enterprise (making contact with the local people) can be thought about as inextricably linked with the success of another (gathering a large collection of plant and animal specimens), or vice versa.

'The failure of communication that had taken place here', which was painfully underlined by the complete absence of the local people on this last day, troubled Cook. Into the emptiness of the final day, this day-without-encounter, he filled the space in his journal with descriptions of what he had been able to learn about the place and its people over the course of the week. It is a postcard from the expedition's first stop on the coast of New Holland: a catalogue of sights seen. There are nice descriptions of the landscape, the birds and animals, the soil and trees and the local people, and directions to fellow travellers about how to get there. Yet the sentence that ends his commentary returns to the matter of his and his men's inability to make contact with the local people. 'However', he concluded,

> we could know but very little of their customs as we never were able to form any connections with them, they had not so much as touch'd the things we had left in their hutts on purpose for them to take away.

This is a sentence that candidly admits to the hole at the heart of this landfall. After a week in the place, the local people's customs, which included the really important things like religious beliefs and practices, laws, kinship structures and marriage rules, modes of government and authority, and concepts of property and ownership, remained opaque to the outsiders.

The disclaimer that Cook provides in respect to his knowledge about the ways of the local people is disarming. It is a pin in the side of the puffed-up image of him as an omniscient man, which developed in colonial Australia afterwards and sometimes still reigns. By his own admission, he is far from all-knowing. He is careful to delineate the limits of his learning in this place. By the time he comes to write a fuller report on the local people based on his observations and experiences during landfalls after Botany Bay, he is more speculative and more expansive. But that is still some time away. For now, he has simply made notes on what he has seen, and not seen, in this place. There is not a lot to work with.

The other journal writers on the ship conclude the much shorter accounts that make up their entries for the last day in the bay with similar comments about the failure to form a connection with the local people. Richard Pickersgill, for instance, writes that 'the inhabitants are so shy that we had no kind of intercourse with them'. His ascription of shyness is more sympathetic than Banks' accusation of cowardliness. Immediately after this, and without any punctuation whatsoever to separate one thought or observation from the next, Pickersgill writes 'they us'd to come down every evening arm'd with lances and wooden swords they appeard very thin and had their faces daub'd over with something white'. The absence of intercourse with the local people is *not* the same as the absence of the local people from the scene altogether, which is the impression that some historical treatments give of Cook and company's time in this place. Stephen Forwood, the gunner, likewise conveys in one simple sentence a picture of both presence *and* absence. He writes in his journal,

> During our stay here we saw partys of the Indians several times, but could not come near enough to make any kind of friendship with them but they always made signals for us to be gone.

But on this last day, it seems, it was the local people who had gone.

The meeting between Cook and the local people ended not with a bang (as it had begun) but a whimper. By day eight, after a week in each other's presence, the distance between the strangers and the locals that existed from the outset had not been bridged. No close connections had been formed between the two groups and there was no shared understanding about what had taken place. The strangers had not conquered; the locals had not conceded. Nothing had been settled.

In their decision on this day, day eight, to be *in absentia*, the local people deny this encounter a sure and decisive endpoint. There was no grand finale, no last word spoken, no ultimate gesture made. There was nothing at all that might provide an exclamation mark or a full stop with which to end an account of it.

That is perhaps precisely how it should be. It makes it an encounter without end. This absence of an ending is registered in the ongoing engagement with this event by the generations who lived in its wake. Ever since that quiet last day in Botany Bay in 1770, Aboriginal people in Australia (near to *and* far from Botany Bay, soon afterwards *and* a long time later) have sought in their storytelling to make sense of that strange meeting. In doing so, they keep it open to interpretation, resisting any attempt to close down its meanings or to allow a final word on its implications. Across Australia, they have told stories and painted pictures to explain what they believed happened when Cook and the local people met, and what it means.

And so the empty last day of this encounter in 1770, when the local people were absent and Cook was at a loose end, can be made to resound with what Aboriginal people across many decades have since had to say on the matter. What they have had to say about Cook begins to undo the quietude that seemed to descend on the day before the *Endeavour* sailed.

Never ENDING

Aboriginal people's storytelling across the nineteenth and twentieth centuries and into the twenty-first about the character called Captain Cook and his encounters with the local people ensures that the original encounter does not become dead and buried in the past. This is no closed chapter of history. It is a past that is continually kept alive by constant talk about it. This is 'an obscure event with a long afterlife', to borrow a phrase from the Indian historian Shahid Amin. The character called Captain Cook matters to Aboriginal people because they contend that whatever was supposedly started by that original encounter at Botany Bay in 1770 is still ongoing. As anthropologist Deborah Bird Rose observes, Aboriginal people's storytelling about Captain Cook 'is ongoing because the relationships it describes and analyses are ongoing too'. The original encounter between Cook and the local people represents the beginning of their complex and fraught history of relations with the British colonists who came after him. It is considered foundational to their later experiences and histories. And so, just as settlers have fashioned the character called Captain Cook as a founding figure and the event of his first landing as a founding moment in the histories they tell, so too have Aboriginal people made their own (alternative) foundational histories from the raw materials of his past actions.

In this way, the name 'Captain Cook' is, as Chris Healy observes, 'common to Aboriginal and non-Aboriginal histories', although what his name stands for is quite different in each. Whereas in non-Aboriginal histories it is a name that stands for the origins of British possession of the territory, or for the genesis of the modern Australian nation, for Aboriginal people the name 'Captain Cook' is a 'means of accounting for certain kinds of change and as a metaphor for ethical dilemmas'. Aboriginal people use the character called Captain Cook to tell histories of their relations with white people, to explain their plight under British colonisation, to mark time before and after the arrival of colonists and settlers, and to outline their vision of a future that restores their law and sovereignty, among other things. Yet although he represents different things in different histories, nonetheless, as a shared symbol 'Cook can be considered as a term which creates a possibility of dialogue between Aboriginal and non-Aboriginal ... histories', says Healy. The character called Captain Cook is a conduit for a conversation between Aboriginal people and other Australians about the past, and about what the past means in and for the present.

Perhaps it comes as a surprise that Aboriginal Australians have been so long and so continuously engaged in making their own meanings from the rudimentary fact that once upon a time Captain Cook was here. Or perhaps it is puzzling that Aboriginal people have been so consistently preoccupied with Captain Cook, seemingly more so than with any other historical figure in Australian history. The anthropologist Kenneth Maddock was puzzled by this. He once wondered in print why Aboriginal people had bothered *so* much in their historical storytelling with what he described as the 'mere passage of the *Endeavour* along the coast', but appeared far less concerned with the 'arrival of the First Fleet at Port Jackson, and the spread of colonisation from that and other coastal footholds'. He thought the latter deserved more attention, given that it had greater direct impact on Aboriginal people's everyday lives.

It is probable that Aboriginal people have been preoccupied with Captain Cook precisely because he has held such a prominent place in Australian memorial and historical and popular culture. There seems to have been an endless Australian interest in him, even if the infatuation has waxed and waned over time. Aboriginal people have responded to this in seeking to make their own versions of Australian history plain.

Just as importantly, Aboriginal narratives 'show interpretative respect for the European injunction that "Captain Cook discovered Australia"', and that as 'first discoverer' he assumed the right to take possession of the territory. Aboriginal people take these twin injunctions seriously, and they have addressed them squarely in their histories, especially in the second half of the twentieth century and into the twenty-first, because they cut to the quick of their experience and their status as the original inhabitants of the continent. If these singular acts are what the man known as Captain Cook is famous for in Australian history – if they are the substance of popular portrayals of him – then the fact that he above all other historical figures looms large in the histories that Aboriginal people tell should come as no surprise at all.

The stories that Aboriginal people have long told about Captain Cook connect with the details of the actual encounter at Botany Bay in 1770, but not in a seamless fashion. Like the foundational stories told by settler Australians, the Aboriginal Captain Cook narratives tend not to fit neatly or easily with the contemporaneous records that were produced by the British participants in the encounter. Nevertheless, while oblique – and even a little obscure – in respect to the historical records, they are never completely fanciful or unconnected to the past event that they reference. There is always a point of connection between what is known about the original encounter and the stories that have since been told about it by Aboriginal people, no matter how mythologised they have become or how strange they seem.

Almost without fail, Aboriginal Captain Cook narratives return to the theme of encounter and exchange between Cook and the locals. Whereas settler historical stories tend to minimise the cross-cultural encounters that occurred, other than the tense meeting on the beach during Cook's first landing on the first day, Aboriginal narratives make them more or less the main story. Against a wilful forgetting of the local indigenous people in many Australian histories of Captain Cook, Aboriginal narrators have tenaciously reinserted their presence. They render this event fundamentally as a meeting between locals and strangers, between black and white. Although some Aboriginal narratives are preoccupied with the things that Cook gave to the locals, or with his penchant for using his gun against them, for instance, it's the fact of the meeting that matters. On this score they appear to pull closer to Cook's own preoccupations as expressed in his voyage journal than their settler counterparts do. For this reason, Aboriginal Captain Cook narratives can illuminate the encounter in 1770 in lively and surprising ways. Some do this by drawing attention to details that dropped from view in the insistent settler storytelling about the same past event. Others tug at dangling threads in authorised accounts and weave them into a new story about what had supposedly happened. Almost all reorient the vantage point from which the encounter is viewed to provide a quite different way of seeing it and understanding it.

By making the encounters between people the main theme of their narratives, Aboriginal people bring Cook's Australian history and (inflated) significance back to a human scale. The historian Mark McKenna believes that it is 'basic human encounters that . . . have become especially lost in our past. Not only the forgetting of the violent encounters, but also the forgetting of the stories of human curiosity . . .'. If nothing more, Aboriginal Captain Cook narratives – oral and visual – are reminders that Captain Cook's celebrated Australian history is really a very human history. At its core, it's about people meeting each other across their differences.

And so the ever-expanding archive of Aboriginal Captain Cook oral and visual narratives is an immeasurably rich resource when it comes to writing Australian histories of Captain Cook at the start of the twenty-first century. This treasure trove of stories demonstrates the doggedness with which Aboriginal people have kept alive and open and relevant the past moment when Cook met indigenous people face to face for the first time on the east coast of Australia. They have not allowed this event to become relegated to the past, or to be of merely historical interest, or to belong to non-Aboriginal people exclusively. They *resist* any final pronouncement on the matter. Whatever happened back then, or whatever was inaugurated (or at least imagined to have been inaugurated) in that original meeting, it's not over yet. That is the point of Aboriginal people's persistent and insistent storytelling about the character called Captain Cook.

CAPTAIN COOK *and the problem of things*

In the early decades of the nineteenth century, some colonists living in Sydney were more curious than others to find out what local Aboriginal people recalled about Cook's time at Botany Bay in 1770. Two interested men were Catholic priests, newly arrived in Sydney, both of whom resided at St Mary's near the Domain. John McEncroe (1794–1868) was from Tipperary in Ireland. In 1832, after a stint in the United States, he became the 'official chaplain of the Catholics in Australia'. William Ullathorne (1806–1889) had been born in Yorkshire, England, the same county from which James Cook had hailed. And like Cook he had been to sea; as a young man he was 'apprenticed before the mast'. Ullathorne spent four years at sea, but in 1823 abandoned ships for religion. Ordained in

England in 1831, he arrived in Sydney in February 1833. McEncroe was known for his energy, Ullathorne for his intellect. They were a formidable pair in the early history of the Catholic Church in the colony.

In 1833 or soon afterwards, they became acquainted with an Aboriginal man from Botany Bay whom McEncroe described as about forty years old, 'intelligent' and able to speak 'English well'. The man's brother had been killed 'inside the Domain wall, just opposite St. Mary's' by another Aboriginal man from the Port Stephens area around Newcastle, and the two priests had been the first on the scene. Unfortunately, the priests do not name him. The historian Keith Vincent Smith has suggested he was Mahroot (also known as the Boatswain), who was a known identity around Sydney in this period.

I have not yet been able to find reference to this incident in the records. It appears that the case did not go before the court, which is not unusual for murder or assault cases involving only Aboriginal people in this period. A case very like it had occurred in 1829, when an Aboriginal man known as 'Borrondire' or 'Dirty Dick' had been killed by another Aboriginal man known as Bob Ballard (or Barrett) near what the *Sydney Gazette* described as 'the heaving-down place, under the Domain'. Yet, when the assailant was taken before the Supreme Court of New South Wales on that occasion, the decision reached by the judges was not to prosecute him, on the basis that 'it never has been the practice in this Colony to interfere in the quarrels of the aboriginal natives'. This no doubt explains why the incident that Ullathorne and McEncroe came upon a few years later has left no trace in the colony's law registers. These 'quarrels' among Aboriginal people might have physically taken place within the Sydney settlement or on its peripheries, but they were deemed by the colonial authorities at the time to exist as though in a parallel universe.

Some legal and historical scholars have recently cited the 1829 case, along with some earlier ones and other evidence, to support an argument that there was recognition of Aboriginal people's sovereignty, however uneasily and unevenly, in the early part of the nineteenth century and into the 1830s. The 'plurality of settler sovereignty' is the way that legal historian Lisa Ford describes it. In other words, Aboriginal sovereignty was not cancelled by a single act in either 1770, when Cook took possession of the east coast, or in 1788, when the British colony was established; moreover, British sovereignty in the early colonial period was limited and spatially bounded. For me, the fact that Captain Cook figures in the story of one of these incidents adds a certain twist, particularly in light of later developments in Australia when he would be widely considered implicated in denying indigenous people's rights, if not solely blamed for their loss of sovereignty within their own country. In the early 1830s, however, this view had not yet arisen or gained traction, either among Aboriginal people or the British settlers. That would be a twentieth-century development.

Back at the Domain in the early 1830s, in the wake of the killing of one Aboriginal man by another, McEncroe and Ullathorne had occasion to have 'several conversations' with the dead man's brother. Perhaps scratching their heads for topics of conversation, the priests asked the man 'if he had any recollections of the landing of Captain Cook in Botany Bay?' The Aboriginal man might have been surprised at the priests' question, but does not seem to have been dazed by it because he did indeed have a story ready to tell. We know its details because each priest later penned an account of it, both of which were eventually published. McEncroe's version was contained in a letter published in the *Sydney Morning Herald* in late April 1863. He had written the letter containing the narrative to Dr Henry Grattan Douglass. Like McEncroe, Douglass hailed from Tipperary. He had been an original member of the Philosophical Society of Australasia in the 1820s, which had been responsible for fixing a plaque to a cliff face at Botany Bay to commemorate James Cook and Joseph Banks' arrival. By the early 1860s, he was involved in reviving the Philosophical Society (as the Royal Society of New South Wales) and organising more commemorative activities of Cook's arrival at Botany Bay. Father Ullathorne's version of the story was included in his memoirs, which he penned in 1867 although they were not published until 1891, not long after his death. The two versions concur in most respects.

In response to their inquiry, the Aboriginal man told Ullathorne and McEnroe that he had not witnessed the arrival of Cook at Botany Bay in 1770 because he had not been born then. But he said that his father had, and that he would tell them what he had heard from him. McEncroe prefaced his transcription of the account with the comment: 'I felt as curious to know his account as he seemed favourably inclined to give'. The man began his narrative by saying that the men who saw the ship arrive had thought it 'was a big bird that came into the bay, and they saw something like opposums running up and down about the legs and wings of the bird'. Ullathorne's version adds the detail that it was the sailors' pigtails that gave the impression of long-tailed possums. The man continued his narrative by saying that 'on viewing them closer they thought them to be people something like themselves'. On this count, the story has something in common with the eyewitness report from the six men that had apparently been collected in the early part of the nineteenth century. In that report, you may remember, the six Aboriginal eyewitnesses had also thought on first sight that the ship was a bird but later decided it was a 'large canoe'. And they had likewise quite quickly identified the figures on board the strange vessel *as people* – not animals, and certainly not spirits, or gods, or ghosts even.

After establishing that the strangers entering the bay were not possums but people, the next part of the Aboriginal man's inherited narrative as transcribed by McEncroe describes what supposedly happened when the seaborne strangers came onto land:

> [The local people] *kept away for a few days without coming near the people who came from the ship to land, although these people made several signs to the natives, who were lurking about the bushes, to come near them. At last it was agreed that two of the tribe would go down and meet the newcomers; but they were directed by the women particularly, when going down to the water, not to eat or drink anything that the strangers may give them for fear of being poisoned.*

This part of the narrative alludes to behaviours recognisable on both sides of the original encounter, as it had been described by Cook and others in their journals. The voyagers' habit of signing to the locals; the local people's practice of keeping their distance; the two men going forward ahead of the rest to meet the strangers; the women staying out of sight; the local people's suspicion of the strangers' things – all of these elements are evident in the voyagers' descriptions of what happened during their time ashore. Superficially, at least, this gives the impression that the Aboriginal man's narrative is about Cook's encounter with the local people at Botany Bay in 1770.

Yet from this point onwards, the narrative begins to deviate in quite obvious ways from the known details of the past encounter. McEncroe's recorded version of it continues in this way:

> *Several of the people from the ship went to meet the two natives, and showed every sign of friendship towards them; one offered a jacket to the natives, which one put on, but when he found himself so cramped in it he threw it off; another gave them a piece of bread or biscuit, which the native chewed and threw out of his mouth and said it was like sawdust; then they showed them a tomahawk and cut down some of the bushes*

with it, the two natives were delighted with this, as it would help them very much in cutting down wood to make gunyahs and spears. One of the sailors then put something into a vessel and drank it off, and wanted the natives to take some of the drink; they were very anxious to get it, but they were afraid of going against the 'gins" advice to eat or drink nothing the strangers would give them. They then consulted what they had best do to get the tomahawk, and they said that as the drink did not kill the stranger who took it it was not likely to kill them and they made signs to the sailor to put more drink into the vessel and drink some of it himself, and they would take the rest; and then they considered that the drink would not kill them if it did not kill the stranger first. The sailor did as directed; he took some of the drink, was quite merry, and gave them the tomahawk, upon which one of them took some of the drink out of the vessel, and he had hardly done so when he thought he was burning alive, and cried out to his companion in his own language: 'Fire in eyes, fire in nose, and fire all over', and ran off to throw himself into the water to quench the fire.

There was not, as far as it is possible to tell from the records, any one episode of gift-giving on the beach during Cook's encounter like the one described here. If there had, it's likely that it would have been written down. And while Cook certainly distributed all manner of things liberally during his time in the bay, it is not clear that any of those items was a jacket, biscuit, axe or alcohol. The items that Cook mentioned he offered were nails, beads, cloth, looking glasses and combs. He described Lieutenant Hicks offering 'presents', but this was probably more of the same. Consistently during Cook's time in their country, the local people did not accept the things offered to them, or express much desire for them. So the narrative is clearly not a straightforward account about Cook's gift-giving on the beach in 1770, even though he is the main character in it.

Although the specificities of the Aboriginal man's narrative do not correspond exactly with Cook's own account, it is possible that the narrative contains a residue of eyewitness accounts passed down orally. More obviously, though, the man's account of the arrival of Cook has become mixed up with other meetings with other strangers on other beaches, so it's a melange of experiences but told as a single narrative structured around the character called Captain Cook. For instance, the whole incident described in the Aboriginal man's narrative has similarities with a situation that Philip Gidley King of the first fleet described in his journal. A couple of days after the fleet had arrived in Botany Bay in the middle of January 1788, there was a situation in which a group of local people received presents offered by Captain Phillip. As King explains it,

> they came round ye boats, and many little things were given them; but what they wanted most was ye great-coats and clothing, but hatts was more particularised by them, their admiration of which they expressed by very loud shouts whenever one of us pulled our hats off.

The gift-giving continued, but King says that he

> found it necess'y to put a stop to our generosity, as they were increasing fast in numbers, and having only a boat's crew with me I was apprehensive that they might find means to surprise us, as every one of them were armed with lances and short bludgeons.

At this point, King explains, 'I gave two of them a glass of wine, which they had no sooner tasted than they spit it out'.

A similar interest in coats is recorded by the surgeon John White in March 1788, when during a meeting between Governor Phillip and a group of local people from either around Botany Bay or Port Jackson 'one of the females happened to fall in love with his great coat', and went to some trouble to get hold of it. An example of a local man finding the experience of wearing clothes for the first time uncomfortable and restricting is recorded by William Bradley. Describing what happened when he gave a local man a shirt, Bradley wrote: 'this skin he seem'd much pleas'd with, but appeared to be deprived of the use of his limbs while in it'.

Likewise, an incident involving the rejection of unfamiliar food, similar to the one described by King, is recorded by the navigator Matthew Flinders during an encounter on a beach on the far south coast of New South Wales in late 1798. While the mariners were taking measurements on the shore, a local man

> of middle age, unarmed, except with a whaddie, or wooden scimitar, . . . came up to us seemingly with careless confidence. We made much of him, and gave him some biscuit; he in return presented us with a piece of gristly fat, probably of whale. This I tasted; but watching an opportunity to spit out when he should not be looking, I perceived him doing precisely the same thing with our biscuit, whose taste was probably no more agreeable to him, than his whale was to me.

And, not surprisingly, similar incidents that register the local people's desire for the newcomers' technology are littered throughout the early colonial archive. Captain Phillip, for instance, reports rewarding an old man with 'a hatchet' and other small things for the kindnesses he had extended to him in the first few weeks of arrival, but there are many other examples when the local people did not wait for the colonists' largesse and took spades and axes when they pleased. These are just a few select examples drawn from the early records that chime with elements in the Aboriginal man's story told to the two priests in 1833 or thereabouts. Further reading through the colonial archive would certainly turn up more.

This archival evidence gives sustenance to the idea that the seemingly strange story is not so strange after all. It is an amalgam, or a montage, of incidents from different times and different places, which have become telescoped, condensed and conflated into a singular moment involving a singular man. This is a classic case of translating the confusion and complexity of past (and indeed present) experiences into a memorable, coherent and repeatable narrative. It is akin to the ways in which the single event known popularly as Captain Cook's 'first landing' came to stand in for a long and complex history (that post-dated the event) of the messy and morally ambiguous means by which the British got the land. This type of conflation and condensation is common in historical mythologising and is one way in which retellings about past experiences become simplified over time. As they continue to be shared between people and across generations, these stories become increasingly stylised and symbolic because it is the meaning that matters more than the details.

In this Aboriginal man's narrative, the character called Captain Cook encapsulates the historical experiences when the local people encounter outsiders and their things. This in turn can be interpreted as a larger symbolic story about the nature of the relationship between the locals and the newcomers and the ways in which things (or goods or commodities) structure that relationship. Associating Captain Cook with this particular historical process is not completely fanciful, given that Cook *did* introduce new things into the local culture, even if they were not the things mentioned in the narrative or were not given in the mode described. And so just as noteworthy as the divergence of the Aboriginal man's narrative from the historical record of what happened in 1770 is, in my view, its fidelity to it.

In a general sense, the man's narrative is loosely faithful to what is known about the past event. If there is one consistent thing that Cook and his crew did over the days they spent ashore in their many dealings with the local people, it was to give gifts. In face-to-face encounters, they invariably offered presents to the local people; or if the locals were nowhere to be seen, they left things lying about their hearths in the hope that they would take them. The strangers had begun doing this from the very start as they attempted to make their first landing. It was their default position on days in between when groups of local men approached them boldly. And they continued as they had begun up to the very end when, for instance, on the penultimate day the officer who stumbled across the old man and the old woman did not know what else to do but to offer them the shot bird in his hand, which 'they would not touch'. By the time the Endeavour sailed away, the local landscape must have been scattered with little piles of little things that Cook and his company had distributed in their attempts to make contact with the local people. That was the detritus of this particular encounter. With his penchant for presents, it's perhaps not surprising that by the 1830s, if not earlier, the character called Captain Cook should become synonymous with the introduction of items from European culture into the local one. He had played an initiating role in that process. What he had begun, others continued.

If the man's narrative was in a general sense loosely faithful to the particular past it purported to be about, then it also had something in common with the image of Captain Cook that had currency among colonists in the period when the narrative was told. For colonists living on the edge of empire in the early nineteenth century, Cook was viewed (among other things) as the harbinger of European civilisation in the antipodes. After his death in 1779, Captain Cook's 'travels were cast as humanitarian acts of civilisation'. Included in these humanitarian acts of civilisation was the bestowing of European goods upon the 'natives' he encountered in his voyages. 'In European history', writes Healy, 'the distribution of trinkets on the beach is the classical act of an explorer's good intentions and kindness'. Educated men living in this distant colony at the beginning of the nineteenth century looked back to Captain Cook as the embodiment of Enlightenment ideals upon which they wished to model their own society and selves. They honoured Cook for his courage and his charity.

The Aboriginal man's narrative, shared with the priests, articulates with aspects of this impression of Captain Cook, so the story itself is an example of an exchange between Aboriginal people and colonists of ideas about and imagery of the same historical figure. However, through processes of exchange, as those images and ideas were transported from one culture to another, their meanings and values were changed. Certainly, the narrative that the Aboriginal man told concentrates on Cook-as-the-giver-of-things, but it destabilises the notion that this was an unmitigated good. In this narrative, the value of the things introduced from Cook's culture to the local one is questioned. The clothes and the food (made from crops), which are markers of European civilisation, are rejected outright. The tomahawk, which is desired because it could contribute to the local people's labour, is shown as coming potentially only at a high cost to the recipients.

The complex experiences that are condensed in this simple narrative about a series of gifts from Captain Cook to the local people belong to the colonial period more so than to the *Endeavour*'s fleeting visit, which occurred at an earlier time. In a stylised and memorable way, the narrative is about the ways in which 'things' introduced by Europeans (or by the British) came to structure relations between Aboriginal people and colonists around Sydney from 1788 onwards. It is a snapshot of the start of a desperate dependence in which there is no reciprocity, no equal exchange and no balance between those who give and those who accept. It is a meditation on what happens when things from outside a culture, out of place and out of context, are improperly introduced. It is a picture of a Faustian bargain struck. The perceptive Father William Ullathorne was alert to the narrative's pathos. He ended his account of it with the observation that: 'Thus the first gift they saw the value of was the axe that was destined to clear their woods and to make way for the white man'.

In the Aboriginal man's narrative, the character called Captain Cook and his men disrupt the existing order. 'By definition', writes Healy, 'a disruption cannot come from the land, because all the relationships of the universe are guaranteed in the land and through the Law'. The gift-giving they commence on the beach – beaches being places of beginnings and endings, as Greg Dening has memorably described them – is askew. Exchange with outsiders who appear in one's territory uninvited is dangerous, because there is no shared framework between the two parties involved. The story is a story of inequality. From a local perspective, Captain Cook had not established his authority to give things; the local men were unwise in accepting things 'out of place'. Things are given to the local men, but oddly they give nothing in return. This imbalance is ominous. Embedded in this early colonial narrative, then, is a theme that will characterise Aboriginal people's perspectives on Captain Cook over the decades that follow. Their narratives will continually point to the ways in which the basis of the relationship between Cook-as-the-original-white-man and Aboriginal people in this country was and is not an equal, balanced, mutual or reciprocal one. As Healy notes in relation to later Aboriginal Captain Cook narratives, in them Captain Cook appears 'as a bearer of immanent structural inequality'. In this schema, there was nothing benign or charitable about the things he gave.

As an account of the nature of the encounter at Botany Bay in 1770, the narrative is only vaguely accurate. As a snapshot of the experience of Aboriginal people in Sydney in the early 1830s, it's very believable. In the 1830s, when this story was first recorded, the general experience of Aboriginal people living in or on the fringes of the settlement of Sydney (and indeed further afield) could easily be encapsulated by reference to the disruption caused by white men coming from the sea bringing things from their own culture. Since 1788, Aboriginal people had lived with them in a structure of inequality, increasingly dependent on the newcomers' handouts and alienated from their own local economies. If the man who had told this story to the two priests in 1833 was indeed Mahroot as Smith suggests, then he appears again in the colonial record ten or so years later giving a more matter-of-fact account of relations between Aboriginal people and white men around Sydney. In his testimony to the Select Committee on the Aborigines held in Sydney in 1845, Mahroot explained the staggering drop in numbers of Aboriginal people living at Botany Bay in the fifty years since he was a boy at the turn of the century. He blamed alcohol as a major cause of his people's demise. Confirmation of his assessments can be found in many visual renditions of the situation: in the caricatures of Aboriginal men and women in ensembles of European dress drinking and dancing in the streets of Sydney or in Augustus Earle's celebrated portrait of Bungaree painted in 1826, which shows him in a hand-me-down red coat.

In this respect, the narrative is 'an impressing of the past into the service of a particular reading of the present'. The Aboriginal man's narrative is offered as a powerful commentary on the times within which he shares his story. When the two priests asked the Aboriginal man in 1833 what he knew about the arrival of Captain Cook at Botany Bay in 1770, they got a picture in words that told them less about that past event and more about the sort of place into which they themselves had recently arrived.

TERRIBLE *hard biscuits*

If the Aboriginal man's story about the arrival of Captain Cook in 1770 was an index to the experience of Aboriginal people in Sydney in the early 1830s, then it appears to have retained some of its relevance for at least another hundred and twenty years or so. In the early 1950s a poet and writer from Sydney, Roland Robinson, hopped on his motorbike and headed for the south coast of New South Wales. In making this and many other trips that followed he was, he said in his autobiography published years later, 'following an intuition I had about finding Aboriginals on the south coast who could tell me something about the past. I might even, I thought, find myths of the country'. He was in search of stories.

On one occasion, while camped on a property on the Tuross River near Bodalla, Robinson visited the 'caste-Aboriginals' as he called them, who were living in shacks nearby while engaged in bean-picking. As he tells the story, he bowled up one evening to the temporary settlement and 'plunged straight into the matter of any of them knowing anything about their stories of the past'. Shakes of the head and silence greeted his question, he claimed, but he offered an open invitation to the Aboriginal men to visit him at his camp if any of them wanted to have a yarn. One man, by the name of Percy Mumbulla, took up his offer, venturing down to Robinson's campsite the following evening. It was the beginning of what would be a long friendship between the two men. A photograph of Percy Mumbulla taken by Lee Chittick in 1978 shows him in the bush near Culburra on the south coast of New South Wales standing confidently, speaking to the camera as though in the middle of an oration (Plate 23).

In the course of that friendship, Percy Mumbulla told Roland Robinson many, many stories, which Robinson transcribed and published as poetry and prose, including one about Captain Cook. In that story, 'when [Captain Cook] landed, he gave the Kurris (Aboriginals) clothes, an' them big sea-biscuits. Terrible hard biscuits they was'. Sound familiar? On this score, it's like the story that the priests had heard in the early 1830s. But unlike that story, in this one food and clothes were all that Captain Cook and his men offered. There was no axe or alcohol anywhere to be seen.

The attitude of the local people in this story to the clothes and the biscuits had not changed over time. The story continued,

> When [Cook and his men] were pullin' away to go back to the ship, them wild Kurris were runnin' out of the scrub. They'd stripped right off again. They was throwin' the clothes an' biscuits back at Captain Cook as his men was pullin' away in the boat.

They did not want the things that Captain Cook gave them; they took the clothes off and spat out the biscuits and threw them back out to sea.

It is impossible to know the precise connection between this story shared in the early 1950s and the one told in the early 1830s, but the later story narrated by Percy Mumbulla begins with an abbreviated account of its lineage that helps to date it, however imprecisely. According to the version that Mumbulla told Robinson, the story had originated with an old Aboriginal woman called Tungeei who had lived at Ulladulla on the New South Wales south coast. 'She was over a hundred, easy, when she died', Mumbulla explained at the outset of the narrative. Before she died, she passed the story on to Mumbulla's father, who was known as King Jacky Mumbulla and lived at the Wallaga Lake Aboriginal settlement on the south coast. He in turn passed it on to his son Percy, who finally decided to share it with Roland Robinson, who wrote it down and published it. Based on the lineage embedded in the narrative itself, it is reasonable to assume that the story dated back to the middle of the nineteenth century, and so not very long after the two priests had heard a more elaborate version of it.

If nothing more, the obvious parallels between the two stories separated by a hundred and twenty years, and at least three generations, is a testament to 'the tenacity of tradition and the reach of memory' among Aboriginal people who were living in the most intensely colonised part of the country. Through that story, the character called Captain Cook had been preserved in the guise of a historical figure best known among Aboriginal people for introducing things that they did not want. Little, it seemed, had changed from one century to the next in Aboriginal people's apprehension and assessment of him. His encounters with Aboriginal people continued to be cast in terms of the things, mostly unwanted, that he bestowed upon them. This is a theme that continues in later Aboriginal narratives about Captain Cook, although in some his gift-giving is portrayed more positively. In a narrative from central Arnhem Land in the Northern Territory, which in 1988 was filmed being told as it was painted onto bark, the character called Captain Cook introduces such items as 'material stuff, blankets, calico'. 'Axes, steel knives; all came from Captain Cook', the narrator Paddy Fordham Wainbarrunga explains. Captain Cook introduced paddles too. All of these things were considered good things, desirable things, useful things.

In the second half of the narrative, the gift-giving Captain Cook is contrasted with men who live after him and who seek to make themselves in his image. 'I've finished with the story of the old Captain Cook. I'm talking now about all the new Captain Cooks', the narrator says to introduce the shift (temporal and otherwise) in the story. People 'started thinking they could make Captain Cook another way', he continues. In this later period there is not one original Captain Cook, but many Captain Cooks – 'Too Many Captain Cooks', as the title given to the story suggests. It is these Captain Cooks 'who have been stealing all the women and killing the people. They have made war. Warmakers, those New Captain Cooks... These New Captain Cooks shot the people', the narrative continues. These corrupt versions of the original Captain Cook do not respect Aboriginal people's law, and they interfere with their affairs. They are the settlers, and the pastoralists, and the welfare mob, who 'wanted to take all of Australia. They wanted it, they wanted the whole lot of this country', the narrative concludes. This is an image of Captain Cook not as a giver but as a taker, and one that resounds loudly with the characterisation of Captain Cook that can be found in some Aboriginal narratives told publicly during the land rights era of the late 1960s and early 1970s, which coincided with the national commemorations of the bicentennial anniversary of Captain Cook's arrival in Australia in 1770.

On not *saying hello*

In April 1970 Hannah Middleton, a student anthropologist from England, arrived at Dagu Ragu (now written as Daguragu) in the Northern Territory to undertake a period of fieldwork with the Gurindji people as part of her research into their struggle for civil and land rights. Later that same month, the two-hundredth anniversary of Cook's first landing at Botany Bay on 29 April 1770 was commemorated in grand style in Sydney. To mark the historic event, a re-enactment of the landing was staged on Botany Bay's southern shore, performed by a cast of Aboriginal and non-Aboriginal actors. Produced expressly for television, but performed in front of members of the British Royal Family and a large live audience, the re-enactment of Cook's initial entry into the local people's territory received widespread media coverage, not only on television but also in the newspapers and on the radio.

As is the case with most historical re-enactments, the organisers took the trouble to stage the past event with as much accuracy as possible. This involved acting out the scene of the first landing faithfully to descriptions made by Cook, Banks and others. Performed for the cameras was the attempt by Cook and Tupaia to speak to the local people gathered on the beach; the offering of some gifts to them; and the firing of guns at them. With the coast made clear by the departure of the local people from the beach, the ersatz landing party stepped ashore. They were immediately joined by many schoolchildren from many different backgrounds in a dance to celebrate the 'young' and 'diverse' national community. Yet again, by stepping ashore, Captain Cook had apparently inaugurated the history of Australia.

Not very long after arriving at Daguragu in April 1970, Hannah Middleton attended a public meeting in the community at which the Gurindji people's claim for rights to their land was being discussed. A local Aboriginal man whom Middleton referred to as Hobble Tanaieri addressed that meeting by telling a story about Captain Cook along with that equally famous Australian historical figure, Ned Kelly. This is Middleton's transcription of Tanaieri's short, spoken narrative:

> First there was water here and then it went back so that there was the Northern Territory. Then a thousand million Aborigines were here and lived on the land for a long time. The first cudeba (white-man) who came was Ned Kelly and he brought with him the first horses, a stallion and mare, who bred here and the first bullock, a very hairy one whose picture you can see on some rocks in Victoria River Downs country. Ned Kelly was a friend of and helped the Aborigines. The second cudeba who came was Captain Cook. He looked at the land and saw that it was very good and wanted it for himself. He decided to clear the Aborigines off the land. So he shot many of them and he shot Ned Kelly too and he stole the land. But now we want the land back!

The last line – 'But now we want the land back' – would become the title of the book Middleton published on her research in 1977, and the story would appear as the book's foreword.

In this narrative, the mantle of the original-white-man-to-introduce-new-things (hoofed animals, in this instance) to Aboriginal people has been given to the character called Ned Kelly, and the character called Captain Cook has been assigned a less flattering status as the original-white-man-to-take-the-land from the Aboriginal people. The characterisation of Captain Cook first and foremost as a land-grabber was prominent in Aboriginal people's public histories throughout the closing decades of the twentieth century, and continues to be so in the opening years of the twenty-first. It has been especially pronounced in the narratives that Hobble Tanaieri continued to tell until the late 1980s.

In September 1980 Deborah Bird Rose, an anthropologist from North America, arrived at Yarralin in the Northern Territory to carry out fieldwork with the local Aboriginal people. 'Virtually from my first day in Yarralin', she later wrote, 'Hobbles [Danayari or Danaiyarri] had been telling me about Captain Cook and the hidden history of the north'. This was the same man whom Hannah Middleton had heard publicly recount his succinct Captain Cook narrative at nearby Daguragu a decade earlier, although the two anthropologists spell his name differently. Rose described Danaiyarri as the 'most philosophically gifted of Yarralin and Lingara historians'. A photograph of him taken by her in the early 1980s captures his thoughtful but steely gaze from beneath his stockman's hat (Plate 24). Early on in her stay in the community, she taped a short version of Danaiyarri's Captain Cook narrative. A year or so later she asked him 'if he would tape the story of Captain Cook again'. This time he told a very long and wide-ranging narrative. Rose explains,

> When [Hobbles] came around ready to begin taping he had prepared in his mind a complete narrative of his understanding of the history of the [local] area, from the first Europeans to the pastoral strikes of the 1960s and 1970s.

His sweeping history, like many Australian histories, begins with Captain Cook. In the beginning was Captain Cook. 'Long way back beginning, I think, right back beginning', says Danaiyarri.

Danaiyarri opens his recorded narratives, both short and long, by introducing himself. 'Right. Well, I'm speaking today. I'm named Hobbles Danaiyarri, and I got a bit of troubling.' A little further on he describes it as 'the biggest troubling', immediately after which he launches into a description of what happened when Cook first arrived in Australia from England. He locates the action at Sydney Harbour, not Botany Bay, but that's inconsequential. In his version of Australian history Captain Cook came to Australia from Big England 'thinking about to get more land'. Cook was a sailor hungry for land. 'Lotta man in Big England, and they start there looking for 'nother land', Danaiyarri says, reducing the history of the complex origins of British colonisation of Australia to one simple statement. Captain Cook and his crew came in a 'sailing boat' to 'have a look at it: Australia', he explains. This portrayal of the purposes of Captain Cook's voyage to Australia as a reconnaissance mission in search of territory suitable for dumping people from overcrowded England echoes popular twentieth-century historical understandings. Commonly, in both serious historical texts and popular imagery, Captain Cook's voyage was cast as the advance party in search of a good place for later colonists to settle. More emphasis tended to be paid to his assessment of the country than to his voyaging or to his dealings with the local people. With these representations circulating throughout the twentieth century, it's not difficult to see why Danaiyarri conceptualised the character called Captain Cook in the way he did.

The portrayal of Captain Cook as hungry for land must also be understood as reflecting the context within which Danaiyarri composed and narrated his histories. These narratives emerged within the context of Aboriginal people's struggles for land rights, a struggle in which Danaiyarri was actively and intimately engaged. The effort to make sense of and to explain in comprehensible ways the process by which Aboriginal people had had their rights to land taken away in the first place was a crucial aspect of the political and legal struggles to have them restored. As many commentators have noted, the name of Captain Cook became shorthand among Aboriginal people for 'a large set of people, processes and regulations' that had dispossessed them of their territory. 'Captain Cook' was a catch-all term for the entire history of dispossession across two hundred years. Billy Gibbs, an Aboriginal man from the Western Desert, used the name 'Captain Cook' in a similar way in this succinct account:

> When Captain Cook came to this land he had a look and said it was an empty land. He took the land through the white law. But the land was there with the Martu law. Captain Cook split the people up. But all the people were still here. Captain Cook made the country a different story.

Throughout this period it was widely believed by most Australians that Captain Cook was single-handedly responsible for the singular act that made the country a British acquisition, and he still often is, despite the best efforts of many historians over the last thirty or so years to debunk or at least unsettle that notion. 'The generally accepted view is that Australia became British by "discovery" as a result of Cook's voyage along the east coast in 1770', wrote the eminent historian Henry Reynolds in his influential book *The Law of the Land*. That this was so helps to explain why Captain Cook was a central figure in Aboriginal histories of how Aboriginal people lost their lands.

In Hobbles Danaiyarri's historical narratives, the presence of the local people *is* paramount. As he tells the tale, the country that Captain Cook was shamelessly eyeing up was a peopled landscape, not an empty one. More than peopled; it was very well populated, in fact. 'And lotta people, lotta women, lotta children, they're owning that city', Danaiyarri explains. In one version of his narrative, he presents a short scenario in which Captain Cook, after favourably assessing the country as 'pretty' and 'good', asks: 'Any more people around here?' 'Yeah, plenty people round here in Sydney Harbour', is the reply. To clarify where the plenty people are, the explanation is given that: 'That mob still in the bush, looking for a bit of fish and tucker'. Just because Cook does not see them does not mean they do not exist. The strong presence of the local population in Danaiyarri's narratives contrasts with their almost complete absence in descriptions of Cook's excursions on the Australian east coast, particularly at Botany Bay, included in many professional and popular Australian history texts produced in the twentieth century.

Danaiyarri's statements about the presence and plenitude of the local people do not only unsettle historical representations of the arrival of Cook in Australia. They can also be interpreted as engaging with (even talking back to) notions such as *terra nullius*, which were never very far away from the figure of Captain Cook in the period during which Danaiyarri developed his interpretations of Australian history generally, and the history of his own people more specifically. *Terra nullius* is a fraught and controversial term in Australian public debate and various historians, legal theorists, journalists, commentators and others argue over its relevance or otherwise to interpreting Australia's history. The debates can be arcane in detail and *ad hominem* in argument, but they nonetheless deal with the very meaty matters of the means by which Aboriginal people were denied rights to their land and the process by which the British assumed ownership of it. Because it is now part of the baggage that his name carries, it is impossible to ignore the topic of *terra nullius* in discussions about Captain Cook's significance in Australian history and memory.

The concept of *terra nullius* became part of that baggage when it was assumed or argued erroneously that Cook took possession of the east coast of New Holland in 1770 for Britain on the basis that it belonged to no-one, as that principle was understood in European legal traditions of the seventeenth and eighteenth centuries. This understanding of Cook's original act of possession gained currency as colonists in the nineteenth century scratched around for justifications that would provide legal and moral weight to Britain's questionable acquisition of the continent. 'By relating the dispossession of the Aborigines to [Cook's act of possession in 1770]', writes Reynolds, 'many moral and legal difficulties appear to have been resolved'. This mode of thought was, in other words, a convenient truth. More than anything, it served to lift the burden of responsibility for the dispossession of Aboriginal people from the shoulders of colonists (who were directly involved) to the shoulders of an imperial navigator called

Captain Cook. Whatever acts of dispossession had taken place, they had supposedly happened before the colonists arrived on the scene, or so went the story that came to hang on Cook's Australian episode. This displacement of dispossession onto a period before the settlers arrive, condensed into a single act (as opposed to a messy and complex process), explains in part the increasing popularity of Cook's first landing as a foundational moment in Australian history. Its popularity grew in the period after the colonial frontier had drawn to a close – at least along the east coast – which was a time when Australians preferred to forget the violence that had been at the heart of earlier relations with Aboriginal people.

As though directly addressing the *terra nullius* argument, Hobbles Danaiyarri points out not only that the country was populated when Cook arrived, but also that the evidence of its ownership by the local people was plain to see. As Rose illustrates, Danaiyarri presents the character called Captain Cook as *someone in the know*. Through his descriptions, he makes it abundantly clear that the figure of Captain Cook had access to all the information he needed in order to know that the Aboriginal people he met were the owners of the place. Glossing Danaiyarri's narrative, Rose explains that: '[The character called Captain Cook] met people living in the country, eating food from the country and demonstrating their superior knowledge of the country . . .'. She continues:

> In Yarralin people's thinking he could not have failed to realise that he was dealing with people who had an undeniable moral right to be where they were. Nor could he have failed to realise the undeniable fact that he did not have the right to be there. His denial of Aboriginal ownership was, therefore, not the result of ignorance but of total disregard of fundamental principles.

By casting Captain Cook as knowing rather than ignorant, Danaiyarri refuses to let him off the hook. He anticipates and meets an argument made by the Australian historian Alan Frost a few years later, in which Frost claims that, given what it was possible for Cook to observe of the local people and their practices, his apparently ultimate assessment that the country belonged to no-one (even though Cook never actually claimed this) was impressively accurate. Hobbles Danaiyarri's interpretation suggests the very opposite. He claims that, given what Cook saw, it was impossible not to know that the local people were the owners of and the bosses for the land.

This makes Cook's evident disregard for the local people he met all the more puzzling to Hobbles Danaiyarri and his contemporaries. A refrain running through the narratives is that Captain Cook did not ask the local people if he could enter their territory. Repeatedly, Danaiyarri insists that Captain Cook should have come up to the local people and said 'hello'.

> [He] should have asked him — one of these boss for Sydney — Aboriginal people. People were up there, Aboriginal people. He should have come up and: 'hello', you know, 'hello'. Now, asking him for his place, to come through, because [it's] Aboriginal land. Because Captain Cook didn't give him fair go — to tell him 'good day', or 'hello', you know. Give people a fair go.

On this score, Danaiyarri is insisting upon more than that Captain Cook should have conformed to local protocols, although he is doing that too. His underlying point is not simply that everything would have been all right had Captain Cook followed the local rules. Confirming this, Rose once asked Yarralin people what would have happened if Captain Cook had asked properly to enter the local people's land. 'I was told', she explained

> that either he would have been denied permission and therefore would have gone away, or he would have been allowed to stay but only on terms decided by the owners of country.

The *status quo* would have remained unchanged.

To criticise Cook for 'not saying hello' is to criticise him for not treating fairly, or properly, or with due respect, the local people he met. There was on Cook's part a fundamental and original failure to recognise and acknowledge the local people as people and as the people with authority over the place that Cook wished to enter. At one point in his narrative, Danaiyarri says, 'we all men [human beings]'. Danaiyarri invokes the popular Australian concept of the 'fair go' to express the absence of equality in the way in which the character called Captain Cook (as the original white man) treated the people with whom he came into contact.

There is an odd resemblance between Danaiyarri's description of what happened and what had actually happened in 1770. The failure of Cook to say 'hello' to the local people chimes with the descriptions contained in the contemporaneous written accounts. In this respect, Danaiyarri's narrative works in a way that is similar to the portrayal of the character of Captain Cook as the original gift-giver. It riffs on a quite prominent element in his behaviour at Botany Bay in 1770, but it constructs a completely different history from those raw materials. It's certainly true that what was missing from that first meeting between Cook and the local people was a willingness on Cook's part to acknowledge the authority of the local people to deny him entry to their territory, or to negotiate the terms on which he might enter it. By taking recourse to his gun in order to get ashore, Cook chose not to recognise the authority of the local people, but rather to assert his own.

If in his painting E. Phillips Fox had removed the gun from Cook's hands, then in Hobbles Danaiyarri's narrative sixty or so years later he's got it back and he's using it. 'Now when he been start to knock [kill] my people up in Sydney that means he been start to clean [eradicate] my people', he says. Danaiyarri's narrative suggests that the character called Captain Cook could not have got the land had he not shot at the people. He makes explicit the violence of the situation when Captain Cook first met local people as well as along later colonial frontiers.

According to Danaiyarri's Australian history, from this original arrogant moment a litany of troubles for his people has flowed. The absence of proper recognition is the foundation of relations between blacks and whites that have since followed. It is the source of Danaiyarri's 'troubling'. And it won't end, he argues, until non-Aboriginal people recognise the immorality of the law that Cook imposed from the beginning. The importance of the narrative is not simply its reinterpretation of history. As Deborah Bird Rose argues, the narratives provide a clear philosophical statement about the injustices and inequalities of the present. It uses the past to explain the present and at the same time the narrative is a vehicle for imagining a different future. Towards the end of the narrative, Danaiyarri explains that the future lies in blacks and whites being friends, being mates with each other. The formation of that friendship since Danaiyarri told his story in the 1970s and 1980s has been fraught to say the least, though many Australians found renewed hope for it in the Australian Prime Minister's apology to the stolen generations in particular and to Aboriginal Australians in general at the opening of the Australian Parliament in 2008.

Back to *Percy Mumbulla*

During the 1970s and 1980s Percy Mumbulla, still living on the south coast of New South Wales along which the *Endeavour* had sailed in 1770, developed his own original interpretations about Captain Cook, which pursued themes different from the story he had inherited from his father in the first half of the twentieth century and which he had shared with Roland Robinson in the 1950s. Less concerned with Captain Cook as a giver-of-things, Mumbulla's own Captain Cook stories reflect more upon the violence that had characterised the first face-to-face meeting between Cook and the local people. A close look at the statements and comments he made from time to time about Captain Cook, some of which have been published in a book titled *Travelling with Percy*, reveal his considerable knowledge of the details of Cook's and the local people's actions in response to each other in 1770. This is knowledge that he might have gathered in 1970 and the years leading up to it as the Captain Cook bicentennial celebrations focused attention on the details of what had happened during Cook's first landing on the east coast of the country. In his commentary on Cook, Mumbulla puzzles over the implications of the violence, and the meaning of the local people's alleged 'retreat' in the face of it.

> *Well, now, Captain Cook come here and he could see that fellas was down there and he was talkin' about guns when he seen 'em with spears and things. Well, then, perhaps he might've fired a shot at 'em. He could. He did! He did fire, not perhaps. He did fire shots at our people and our people wasn't goin' to stop there for him to shoot the lot. They just had to vanish and get right back.*

But his story of this encounter does not end here, in the way that the stories told through re-enactment during the 1970 bicentenary typically did. He moves from this point into a discussion about what happened when Captain Cook came ashore and began behaving as if he was the leader, a situation which his narrative resolves in a surprising way:

> *Well, when soon ever Captain Cook come ashore, they didn't know he was Captain Cook until he was takin' the lead. Well, they made a job of spearin' him and they didn't know it was Captain Cook until they found out, Oh, Captain Cook got killed with the blackfellas. Put a spear through him, eh? See? There you are! Yeah, on an island, see. This is the island we're talking about, on this island. This is the island!*

It is difficult not to read this passage without thinking about the death of Captain Cook in Hawai'i in 1779 during his third voyage, where he was killed by the local people during a violent melee. It's impossible to know whether or how much Mumbulla knew about the details of Cook's death to be certain that it infused his own interpretations.

Percy Mumbulla's narrative continues with an explanation of the local people's killing of Captain Cook, which he locates as having happened at Botany Bay.

> *Now, when he come into Botany Bay, he come straight ashore there on Kurnell side. And that's where they blackfellas was along that bay there, right up. And they come right up from Kurnell, from Botany, from Kurnell right around, right up to Cooks River and Mascot. Right up where you come to go up on the Cook River and Georges River, eh?*

See! Well, that's where all the Kooris laid in there, and that's how he come to see 'em. 'Hello!', he must've said. 'Well, there's the blackfellas. Now this is goin' to be a go'. I suppose he must have been tellin' them. 'We'll go up into that bay'.

So when they come into that bay, that's where they must've fired a shot at 'em first to try 'em out. Well, when he fired the shot, that done the damage, see? Well, as soon as they come ashore, well, the first thing they got, then they just got a shower of spears straight at 'em, isn't it? Well, Captain Cook couldn't get away and they didn't know whether it was Captain Cook or who it was. So they just drove the spear and put it right in and that was the end of him, see. When you get those spears, you can't get it out. You have to break it out, or pull your guts out, one of the two, see. Well, that's what they did. That's how they killed Captain Cook.

Mumbulla singles out Cook's 'unprovoked' first shot – a shot that he presents as Cook 'trying 'em out' or 'trying them on' – as the problem. It's the original violence. 'That done the damage, see', he says. He resolves that problem, somewhat wishfully, through a story about retribution, in which Cook's violence is repaid with violence. This restores the order of things, in which it is the local people who are once more the leaders. His story ends here, like his earlier story, with the problem of Captain Cook resolved by his disappearance or departure and with the sovereignty of the country retained by the local people. It has a more utopian ending than some of the other Aboriginal stories told in the same period.

Repainting *history*

While Hobbles Danaiyarri and Percy Mumbulla continued to tell Captain Cook narratives in the 1980s, Brisbane artist Gordon Bennett began producing a series of artworks that incorporated and unsettled popular images of Captain Cook. Bennett's early paintings, produced in the late 1980s and early 1990s, worked from 'the canonical images of Captain Cook and explorers' ships, the foundational moments of possession and the myths of exploration'. They included, among others, a painting titled *Possession Island* (Plate 25), which Bennett worked up from engravings of J. A. Gilfillan's mid-nineteenth century painting *Captain Cook Taking Possession of the Australian Continent on Behalf of the British Crown AD 1770* (Plate 12). Engravings of Gilfillan's painting were in circulation throughout the twentieth century, repeatedly reprinted in school textbooks and Australian history books and on postcards. Like some other artists working in the period around the 1988 national bicentenary, which commemorated two hundred years of European settlement in Australia, Bennett was interested in the visual imagery that was used to convey Australian historical narratives and their moral messages. These were the images designed to instruct Australian schoolchildren in what it meant to be Australian.

In *Possession Island*, as in many other paintings he produced in the same period, Bennett adapted the signature paint dripping and throwing technique of American artist Jackson Pollock. As Nicholas Thomas points out, Bennett's engagement with Pollock's work relates specifically to the American artist's celebrated painting Blue Poles Number 11 (1952). In 1973 the newly elected Australian government under the prime ministership of Gough Whitlam, the first Labor government for more than twenty years, purchased the painting for 1.3 million Australian dollars, a large sum for the federal government to pay for a single artwork at the time, particularly for an abstract painting. Not surprisingly, the painting and its purchase were the subject of vigorous public debate. The Whitlam Labor government wore the painting as a badge of the nation's new openness and expansiveness, and as a marker of the importance it placed on art and culture in renewing Australian culture and society in the 1970s.

Thus, by reworking Gilfillan's *Captain Cook Taking Possession* and by borrowing techniques from Pollock's *Blue Poles*, Gordon Bennett's work engages with two different 'national' pictures – a historical one and a contemporary one. *Possession Island* can be interpreted as a commentary on the ways in which paintings construct narratives of the nation, or become expressions of national identity. By draping an old nineteenth-century history painting that celebrates British possession of the Australian continent in Jackson Pollock signature style drips, Bennett cleverly registers the cultural politics that surround these two paintings in particular, and art practice more generally.

However, that is not the only issue. Bennett applies Pollock's drip technique to his own work in order to express ideas that are central to his repainting of Australia's history. Nicholas Thomas suggests that Gordon Bennett reworked a painting technique usually understood as expressive of the tortured inner life of the individual artist to express instead the troubled psyche of the nation seeking to come to terms with its violent and confused past. In *Possession Island*, the drip technique sends into chaos the neatly ordered landscape that Gilfillan had portrayed in the original painting. Cook and his companions become lost in a maelstrom of swirling paint strokes. The figure holding the flag under which Cook makes his declaration appears to struggle against a storm.

Standing out from this chaotic background is the figure of Tupaia. Bennett has painted him against a perspectival grid. He wears bright, monochromatic clothes. Holding under his arm an ultra-white napkin and carrying a drinks tray, he has been made to look like the figure of the archetypal black man ubiquitous in popular culture and advertising in the first half of the twentieth century. Drawing him into the foreground, Bennett evokes histories of slavery and racism that are at the heart of the histories of empire that Captain Cook embodies, but are hidden in Australian histories that celebrate Cook and his deeds. For Gordon Bennett, the backstory to Cook's achievements is the history of imperialism, slavery and the subjugation of black people by Europeans.

Gordon Bennett's artistic practice, in which he reworks old images in order to reconstitute national narratives, highlights the ways in which it is not just history as past events, but also history as the *story* that is told about those past events, that structures relations between Aboriginal and non-Aboriginal people in Australia. His concern is not so much with what transpired between Cook and the local people on the beach, or indeed with other encounters. Rather, he is interested in the ways in which visual representations of these historical events and processes obscure the hidden injustices inherent within colonial relations. His paintings draw attention to the ways in which Aboriginal people have been oppressed not only by colonial domination but also by the colonists' documentation or representation of history. This is what Chris Healy has referred to as the twin forces of 'domination and documentation'.

WE CALL THEM *pirates out here*

The colours of the clothes are brighter than in the original, but the sky is darker and the clouds more menacing. My eyes are moving back and forth between Daniel Boyd's 2006 painting *We Call Them Pirates Out Here* (Plate 26) and E. Phillips Fox's 1902 painting *The Landing of Captain Cook at Botany Bay in 1770* (Plate 10). Boyd's work imitates and parodies Phillips Fox's earlier piece and so invites 'a game of spot the difference' between the two images produced a century or more apart.

In Boyd's new version of Phillips Fox's old painting Cook, still standing resplendent in the centre, wears a black patch over one eye. A brightly coloured parrot on his shoulder peeps out from behind his hat. Another is sitting on the shoulder of Daniel Solander, who still steps daintily upon the shore. The sailors surrounding Cook and Solander look like a bevy of buccaneers. They are like the pirates with blue-striped pants found in children's picture books. The motley crew stand with their commander on the beach under a Union Jack overlaid with a skull-and-crossbones – a Jolly Jack, as Boyd calls it. In case the viewer has missed the point, the title – *We Call Them Pirates Out Here* – is incorporated in the painting.

Alongside the satirising gestures that change Captain Cook from celebrated founder to commonplace pirate are other less obvious alterations that make poignant points about national history, about art, and about ways of seeing things. Look closely and you will see that the face on the lad holding the flag is different. It is less youthful and not as naively optimistic as the one painted by E. Phillips Fox. I learn later that it is modelled on a friend of the artist, a man who migrated to Australia from England via Scotland. He had taken a journey similar to that of Cook and his crew. The red-coated marine beside the flag-bearer in Boyd's painting is the artist's housemate. By putting his friends in the frame, Daniel Boyd incorporates present-day, personal histories into national history narratives and makes this history seem closer to home. The imagined gap between the past and the present has been narrowed. The artist's non-Aboriginal friends, and by extension non-Aboriginal people in general, become participants in history, not merely the recipients of its imagined legacies. They (we) are actors, not bystanders.

Just as powerfully, Daniel Boyd alters the portrayal of the two local men, who in E. Phillips Fox's painting appear as small, shadowy, barely discernible figures on the edge of the canvas. In Boyd's painting, the pair have lost their human form and been turned into 'black boys', the native plant for which the scientific name is *xanthorrhoea*. This transmutation is loaded with meaning. In particular, by changing the two local men into natural features in the landscape, Daniel Boyd uncovers and unsettles naturalised (that is, accepted) ways of seeing this past event, and of seeing or indeed *not* seeing Aboriginal people more generally.

The representation of two local men as native plants – as an indistinguishable part of the natural landscape – returns us to Cook's alleged failure to recognise the local indigenous people he encountered *as* human. It's an unfair charge in my opinion, but it's an idea that has currency in contemporary views about the character called Captain Cook.

Not acknowledging inherent equality based on shared humanity is a theme in Hobbles Danaiyarri's oral narratives, which is expressed in his insistence that Captain Cook should have said 'hello' to the local people and which he summed up in the comment 'we are all men [human beings]'. Yet, with the two men changed into native plants, Boyd not only makes it appear as though Cook failed to see the local people as sharing his own humanity; rather, he makes it seem that Cook failed to see the local people at all. Cook sees the place as empty of people. The spectre of *terra nullius* haunts the painting, just as it infuses Aboriginal people's Captain Cook stories told since the 1970s.

However, there is more to Boyd's pictorial gesture than this. By turning the local men into native plants, the painting evokes ways of seeing this place primarily as a botanical wonderland. Joseph Banks no longer points with fear in his eyes at the two men who threaten the landing party, but instead at the two strange plants sticking up on the ridge. Celebrating this landscape for its botanical riches (as enshrined in the name 'Botany Bay' bestowed by Cook) is yet another means by which the local inhabitants are made to fade from view. It is a vision that is repeated time and again in later Australian history books, in which Banks' botanical collection is presented as the most important thing to have happened, for instance, or in which Cook is portrayed as interested only in the place and not at all in the people.

But those observations do not exhaust the possible meaning of the gesture either. By turning the two men into 'black boys', Boyd plays around with the history of ideas about and representations of Aboriginal people in colonial Australia. In the colonial vernacular, these plants were called 'black boys' apparently because they were thought to resemble an Aboriginal figure standing on one leg holding an upright spear. It's a caricature. To portray the two men as 'black boys' is to highlight the roles that language and racism played in shaping relations between Aboriginal and non-Aboriginal people in colonial Australia. Boyd may also be suggesting that Cook inaugurated ways of seeing in which local people were simply viewed as part of the flora and the fauna, or as being so close to nature as to be indistinguishable from it.

Like Gordon Bennett before him, Daniel Boyd's artistic practice involves playing around with imagery, ideas, language and perspective in order to make plain the assumptions hidden in iconic Australian history paintings. Boyd is concerned with the ways in which ideas about history

– about ways of seeing past events – are expressed through the visual arts, past and present. He is keenly aware of the historical role that artists play in producing images that structure and shape ideas in Australia and understands the undisputed power of the visual medium for communicating ideas about history, about Aborigines and about encounters between Aborigines and non-Aborigines. 'Questioning the romantic notions that surround the birth of Australia is primarily what influenced me to create this body of work', he explains. He chips away at these romantic notions by disassembling and reassembling old paintings, cleverly retouching some elements, cheekily adding others, until it is impossible to look at the scene in the same way as E. Phillips Fox presented it a hundred years earlier. In the process, a suite of other histories emerges from the ruins of the old painting. They are histories about land taken, about colonial relations, about racism. Over an old historical tableau, Boyd overlays another quite different one, but cut from the same cloth and drawn from the same past event.

Also like Bennett, Boyd is not only concerned with past paintings, but also with the nation's acquisition of new and expensive ones. *We Call Them Pirates Out Here* is not only in conversation with E. Phillips Fox's 1902 picture; Daniel Boyd's foray into painting his series of Captain Cook pictures was triggered by the National Portrait Gallery of Australia's acquisition of John Webber's 1782 *Portrait of Captain James Cook RN* (Plate 27). The National Portrait Gallery purchased the painting in 2000 for the sum of 5.3 million Australian dollars. This was a huge amount of money for a single painting. Two private benefactors contributed handsomely to the purchase price, but it took an additional 2.8 million dollar contribution from the Australian government to secure the painting. The National Portrait Gallery might not have become the repository for the portrait had it not enjoyed strong support for the acquisition of the painting from its patrons, John Howard, then prime minister of Australia, and his wife Janette. As the National Portrait Gallery's director Andrew Sayers explained, John Howard along with others 'felt that the portrait was too significant a work to be allowed to slip from the grasp of the Australia'.

The portrait is considered the National Portrait Gallery of Australia's 'foundation piece'. If E. Phillips Fox's *The Landing of Captain Cook at Botany Bay in 1770* (1902) celebrated the Australian nation at the beginning of the twentieth century, then John Webber's *Portrait of Captain James Cook RN* (1782) celebrated it at the start of the twenty-first. Captain Cook had somehow retained or regained his place as a founding figure in the nation's history.

However, if Cook's national foundational status remained alive, so did Aboriginal people's challenges to it. The purchase of the portrait provoked Nyungar artist Dianne Jones to parody it in her piece entitled LHOOQ 'ERE!, which she produced in 2001 (Plate 28). In it, she adds a moustache and goatee beard to Captain Cook in the style of the French artist Marcel Duchamp's treatment of Leonardo da Vinci's *Mona Lisa*, which carried the inscription L.H.O.O.Q., a pun in French. According to art critic Odette Kelada, 'Jones' art is informed by a politics of transforming and inventing a radical shift in the popular ideologies of Australian representation and cultural identity'. In this piece, she argues, Jones 'points to something ridiculous in its gravity as if to say, come have a look at this – Are they for real? Is this reality?'

Daniel Boyd has also produced his own reworking of the portrait as part of a series of paintings based on old portraits of figures from Australia's colonial history, including King George III, in whose name Cook claimed possession of the east coast of Australia and under whose reign the British established a colony at Port Jackson. In his parody of the portrait by John Webber, which he created in 2005, Boyd presents Cook in the guise in which he appears in *We Call Them Pirates Out Here*, with a patch over one eye and a parrot perched on his shoulder (Plate 29). Boyd has called the painting *Captain No Beard*, a description that he repeats in the other playful portraits he has made of historical figures, including *King No Beard* for King George III and *Governor No Beard* for Governor Arthur Phillip. The 'No Beard' in the name is a play on Black Beard, an English pirate active in the Caribbean in the early eighteenth century. Boyd has said that he draws parallels between 'the act of piracy' and 'nationalistic rivalry' over territory in the imperial age, including Cook's act of taking possession of the east coast of New Holland without the consent of the 'natives'. This same preoccupation is at the heart of his history painting, *We Call Them Pirates Out Here*.

Daniel Boyd frames his painting *We Call Them Pirates Out Here* in a very particular way. Around it he has painted a narrow white border, which makes the image resemble a postcard more than a serious history painting. In the frame along the bottom he has painted the picture's title, *We Call Them Pirates Out Here*, as though it is some cheeky slogan sending up a revered historic tourist site. By using the postcard format, Boyd comments on the constant reproduction of Phillips Fox's original painting and its mass circulation far beyond the confines of an art gallery. Indeed, Boyd himself first saw an image of the painting printed on a postcard. As though answering back to the message written on the original painting, Boyd has sent his own riposte into the world as a postcard from the edge – a message from 'out here', not 'in there'. 'With our history being dominated by Eurocentric views', he explains, 'it's very important that Aboriginal and Torres Strait Islander people continue to create dialogue from their own perspective to challenge the subjective history that has been created'. *We Call Them Pirates Out Here* is part of his contribution to the creation and the continuation of that conversation.

The painting with its title embedded in it plays around with actual and metaphorical locations, or standpoints, or vantage points. The 'here' in Boyd's painting signals not simply the place or territory belonging to the local people that Cook stepped into in 1770; it also registers a contemporary collective Aboriginal standpoint that exists within the wider Australian community, but which is characterised by quite different interpretations of Australia's history compared with more authorised or orthodox accounts.

Captain Cook Was Here.
    We Call Them Pirates Out Here.

The ENDEAVOUR SAILS

*E*arly in the morning after the eerily quiet last day in the bay, the Endeavour set sail. In a slightly contradictory way, given his admission about not being able to form a connection with the local people, Cook wrote in his journal that:

> Having seen every thing this place afforded we at day light in the Morning weigh'd with a light breeze at NW and put to sea and the wind soon after coming to the Southward we steer'd along shore NNE and at Noon we were by observation in the Latitude of 33°50's about 2 or 3 Miles from the land and abreast of a Bay or Harbour wherein there apper[d] to be safe anchorage which I call'd Port Jackson.

There is no mention of any local people lining the headlands to see the ship leave. That is not to say that they didn't witness it. No doubt they watched its departure. If they had used retreat as their final movement in their strategy for dealing with these strangers, then they must have been happy with the seeming speed of its effects.

Away from this place and some time later, the Endeavour's voyage under Cook's command would directly and indirectly set in train a whole series of decisions and events and processes that in a roundabout and unpredictable way would lead to a decision being made in England to establish a colony for convicts at Botany Bay. But that is another story.

Sources

Voyage accounts

Most of the quotes from James Cook and Joseph Banks are from the authoritative published editions of their journals prepared by J. C. Beaglehole.

> Beaglehole, J. C. (ed.), *The Endeavour Journal of Joseph Banks, 1768–1771*, vols. I and II, 2nd edn (Sydney: The Trustees of the Public Library of New South Wales in association with Angus and Robertson, 1963).
>
> Beaglehole, J. C. (ed.), *The Journals of Captain James Cook*, vol. I, *The Voyage of the Endeavour 1768–1771* (Cambridge: Cambridge University Press, 1955).

The other published voyage journal cited is:

> Sydney Parkinson, *Journal of a Voyage to the South Seas* (London: Printed for Stanfield Parkinson, 1773).
>
> Parkinson's journal can also be accessed through The South Seas Project website hosted by the National Library of Australia: http://southseas.nla.gov.au/index_voyaging.html.

In addition to the published version of Cook's voyage journal, I drew from manuscript copies of his journal and logs, including the holograph log held by the British Library in London (Add. MSS 27885) and the holograph journal held by the National Library of Australia in Canberra (MS1). The latter can also be accessed through the National Library of Australia's website: http://southseas.nla.gov.au/index_voyaging.html.

Other manuscript journals and logs compiled on the *Endeavour* include:

> Anonymous, *A log of the proceedings of His Majestyes Bark Endeavour* [26 Aug 1768–28 Sept 1770], ADM 51/4548/155, The National Archives, London.
>
> Bootie, John, *A Journal* [John Bootie 25 Nov 1769–3 Sept 1770], ADM 51/4546/135, The National Archives, London.
>
> Briscoe, Peter, *Log*, MS 96, Dixson Library, State Library of New South Wales, Sydney.
>
> Clerke, Charles, *The Endeavour Journal by Cha. Clerke* [1 Nov 1769–8 June 1770], ADM 51/4548/144, The National Archives, London.

Forwood, Stephen, *A Log of the Proceedings of his Majestys Bark Endeavour Commencing May 27 1768* [–26 Sept 1770] *by Step^n Forwood, Gunner*, ADM 51/4545/133, The National Archives, London.

Green, Charles, [log kept by Mr Charles Green, Astronomer to the expedition 1768–70], ADM 51/4545/151, The National Archives, London.

Hicks, Zachary, *The Endeavour Journal commencing the 20 Novr 1769 & ending 14 March 1771 by Lieut^t Zachary Hickes*, ADM 51/4546/148, The National Archives, London.

Hicks, Zachary, *Log of the Endeavour*, fms-088, Alexander Turnbull Library, Wellington.

Master's Log [Molyneux], *Endeavour* [26 Aug–20 Oct 1769], ADM 55/39, The National Archives, London. Extract published in J. C. Beaglehole (ed.) *The Journals of Captain James Cook*, vol. I, *The Voyage of the Endeavour 1768–1771* (Cambridge: Cambridge University Press, 1955), pp. 551–64.

Molyneux, Robert, *A Journal of the Proceedings of His Majestyes Bark Endeavour Lieut James Cook Commander, R. Molen^x* [27 May 1768–9 Jan 1770], ADM 51/4546/152, The National Archives, London.

Monkhouse, William Brougham, *Journal*, Add. MS 27889, The British Library, London. Extract published in J. C. Beaglehole (ed.) *The Journals of Captain James Cook*, vol. I, *The Voyage of the Endeavour 1768–1771* (Cambridge: Cambridge University Press, 1955), pp. 564–87.

Pickersgill, Richard, *Journal of the Proceedings of His Maj^y Bark Endeavour Lieut^t Ja^s Cook Commander Commencing October the 7th 1769* [–20 Aug 1770] *by Richd Pickersgill*, ADM 51/4547/141, The National Archives, London.

The Ship's Log, Add. MS 8959s, The British Library, London.

Wilkinson, Frank, *No. 2* [Endeavour Journal, 9 October 1769–3 August 1770], ADM 51/4547/150, The National Archives, London.

Other sources

The sources for all other direct quotations in the text are listed below.

In the beginning

p. 4 'Voyagers would stop . . .', Greg Dening, *Islands and Beaches: A Discourse on a Silent Land, Marquesas, 1774–1880* (Melbourne: Melbourne University Press, 1980), p. 23.

p. 5 Email correspondence, Nigel Erskine to author, 2 October 2007.

p. 7 'at least suggestive . . .', Nicholas Thomas, *Discoveries: The Voyages of Captain Cook* (London: Allen Lane, 2003), p. xxxiv.

'a stranger . . . seen . . .', A. W. Howitt, *The Native Tribes of South-East Australia* (first published 1904), facsimile edition. (Canberra: Aboriginal Studies Press, 1996), p. 724.

p. 8 'there was always a fine line . . .', Nicholas Thomas, *Cook's Sites Exhibition Catalogue* (Sydney: Historic Houses Trust, 2006), p. 5.

'9 or 10 of the Natives . . .', William Dampier, *A Voyage to New Holland &c. in the Year 1699* . . . (London: printed for James Knapton, 1703), accessed through Eighteenth Century Collections Online, Gale Group, p. 145.

p. 9 'The Natives as we Sail'd in . . .', extract of letter from David Blackburn to Richard Knight, 12 July 1788, quoted in Philip Jones, *Ochre and Rust: Artefacts and Encounters on Australian Frontiers* (Kent Town, SA: Wakefield Press, 2007), p. 23.

'a Circle of white Paste . . .', Dampier, *A Voyage to New Holland*, p. 147.

'red coats and white crossed belts . . .', *Terra Australis: Matthew Flinders' Great Adventures in the Circumnavigation of Australia*, edited and introduced by Tim Flannery (Melbourne: Text Publishing, 2001), p. 54.

'created a sense of occasion . . .', Sylvia Hallam, 'A view from the other side of the western frontier: or "I met a man who wasn't there . . ."', *Aboriginal History* 7(2) (1983), p. 138.

p. 10 'personal notes . . .', Bernard Smith, 'The first European depictions', in Ian Donaldson and Tamsin Donaldson (eds), *Seeing the First Australians* (Sydney: Allen & Unwin, 1985), p. 28.

'many of their warriors . . .', John White, *Journal of a Voyage to New South Wales by John White Surgeon-General to the First Fleet and the Settlement at Port Jackson* (Sydney: Angus and Robertson in association with the Royal Australian Historical Society, 1962), p. 111.

p. 11 'Each family has . . .', David Collins, *An Account of the English Colony in New South Wales, from its first settlement in January 1788, to August 1801: with remarks on the dispositions, customs, manners, &c. of the native inhabitants of that country* (London: Printed by A. Strahan for T. Cadell and W. Davies, 1798–1802, facsimile edition, Adelaide: Libraries Board of South Australia, 1971), pp. 345–6.

p. 12 'exceedingly ferocious ...', Terra Australis, p. 5.

p. 16 'to stem the continued advance ...', Hallam, 'A view from the other side', p. 150.

A copy of the Earl of Morton's Hints is published in Appendix II, Beaglehole (ed.), The Voyage of the Endeavour 1768–1771, pp. 514–19.

'the hints have ...', Inga Clendinnen, Dancing with Strangers (Melbourne: Text Publishing, 2003), p. 23.

p. 19 'The voyage had passed ...', Thomas, Discoveries, p. 113.

p. 20 'foreshortened the cultural lesson ...', Dening, Islands and Beaches, p. 21.

'we could perceive no arms ...', Terra Australis, p. 11.

'about half an hour ...', W. Baldwin Spencer & F. J. Gillen, Across Australia (London: Macmillan, 1912), p. 249.

'No matter how exercised ...', Dening, Islands and Beaches, p. 18.

'Cook believed that ...', Thomas, Discoveries, p. 92.

p. 24 'intended to honour Federation', Ruth Zubans, E. Phillips Fox: His Life and Art (Melbourne: The Miegunyah Press, 1995), p. 97.

p. 27 'To know history ...', Chris Healy, From the Ruins of Colonialism: History as Social Memory (Melbourne: Cambridge University Press, 1997), p. 20.

'luminous vision' and 'prescient anticipation', Healy, From the Ruins, p. 16.

The script of the 1901 re-enactment was printed in a commemorative booklet The Landing of Lieutenant James Cook, R.N., at Botany Bay (Sydney: W. A. Gullick, Government Printer, 1901), pp. 21–8. All quotations from the performance are taken from it.

p. 29 'one of the best known ...', Bernard Smith, European Vision and the South Pacific, second edition (Melbourne: Oxford University Press, 1989), p. 74

p. 30 'owe their stance ...', Smith, 'The first European depictions', p. 30.

p. 31 'champions', John Hawkesworth, An Account of the Voyages Undertaken by the Order of His Present Majesty for Making Discoveries in the Southern Hemisphere, vol. III (London: Printed for W. Strahan and T. Cadell, 1773), p. 493.

pp. 31 & 32 'establishes an Australian beginning ...' and 'oriented towards ...', Anne Brewster, 'The beach as "dreaming place": reconciliation, the past and the zone of intersubjectivity in Indigenous literature', New Literatures Review 40 (2003), p. 34.

p. 32 Thomas suggests that E. Phillips Fox had borrowed the gesture from John Webber's painting, The Death of Captain Cook, Thomas, Discoveries, p. 412.

pp. 33 & 34 'Objection must ... be taken ...' and 'It is not well ...', Daily Telegraph, 6 September 1902.

p. 35 'A certain amount of poetic license . . .', *The Landing of Lieutenant James Cook, R.N., at Botany Bay*, p. 21.

p. 37 'He who in dispossessing . . .', Healy, *From the Ruins*, p. 29.

p. 44 'from someone who made . . .' and 'it was a particular proposition . . .', Thomas, *Discoveries*, pp. 113–14.

pp. 45ff The testimony from the six local Aboriginal men is printed in Samuel Bennett, *A History of Australian Discovery and Colonisation* (Sydney: Hanson & Bennett, 1865), pp. 83–4. For another mention of some of these Aboriginal men in the early nineteenth century, see *Old and New Sydney*, reprints from the *Sydney Morning Herald* (Sydney: Edward Hordern & Sons, 1882), p. 5.

In between

p. 51 'watering was more involved . . .', Ray Parkin, *H. M. Bark Endeavour: Her Place in Australian History* (Melbourne: Miegunyah Press, paperback edition, 2006), p. 47.

p. 52 'Water in a cask is heavy . . .', Parkin, *H. M. Bark Endeavour*, p. 48.

p. 53 'agency, efficacy, and personality . . .', Denis Byrne, *Surface Collection: Archaeological Travels in Southeast Asia* (Lanham: AltaMira Press, 2007), p. ix.

'The ceremonial context . . .', Sandra Bowdler, 'Movement, exchange and ritual life in south-eastern Australia', in Ingereth Macfarlane (ed.), *Many Exchanges: Archaeology, History, Community and the Work of Isabel McBryde* (Canberra: Aboriginal History, 2005), p. 141.

'Indigenous participation in traffick . . .', Bruce Buchan, 'Traffick of Empire: Trade, Treaty and Terra Nullius in Australia and North America', *History Compass*, 5/2 (2007), p. 391.

p. 54 For Beaglehole's comment that Cook 'writes nonsense about Australian society', see: J. C. Beaglehole (ed.), *The Journals of Captain James Cook*, vol. I, *The Voyage of the Endeavour 1768–1771* (Cambridge: Cambridge University Press, 1955), p. cxcii.

For Williams' discussion on this matter, see: Glyndwr Williams, '"Far more happier than we Europeans": Reactions to the Australian Aborigines on Cook's Voyage', *Historical Studies*, vol. 19, no. 77 (1981), pp. 499–512.

'Banks airs the anxieties . . .' and 'we might guess . . .', Thomas, *Discoveries*, p. 129.

p. 56 'The more likely explanation . . .', Keith Willey, *When the Sky Fell Down: The Destruction of the Tribes in the Sydney Region 1788–1850s* (Sydney: Collins, 1979) pp. 26–7.

'a spirit sent by Turong . . .', Eleanor Dark, *The Timeless Land* (Sydney: Angus & Robertson, 1980, first published New York: Macmillan, 1941), p. 19.

p. 57 'time to assess and discuss . . .', Hallam, 'A view from the other side', p. 142.

SOURCES

143

p. 58 'empowered to make . . .', Hallam, 'A view from the other side', p. 138.

p. 60 'In their gestures . . .', F. Peron, *A Voyage of Discovery in the Southern Hemisphere, performed by order of the Emperor Napoleon during the years 1801, 1802, 1803 and 1804* [1809], facsimile reprint (Melbourne: Marsh Walsh, 1975), p. 71. A new English edition of the second edition of Peron's journal prepared by Christine Cornell and published in 2006 by the Friends of the State Library of South Australia translates this sentence as: 'Their gestures seemed to be telling us to retrace our steps; they even appeared to be pointing out to us the path by which we had come and indicating the one that we supposed also led to the sea' (p. 73).

'The European intruders . . .', Hallam, 'A view from the other side', p. 134.

p. 61 'certain visits by . . .', John Mulvaney, *Encounters in Place: Outsiders and Aboriginal Australians 1606–1985* (St Lucia: University of Queensland Press, 1989), p. 14.

p. 63 'got up and called . . .', King's Journal, *Historical Records of New South Wales*, vol. II, p. 539.

'great noise' and 'terrible tone', Peron, *A Voyage of Discovery in the Southern Hemisphere*, pp. 70 & 71.

'continued to howl . . .', Hallam, 'A view from the other side', p. 153.

Diane Collins, 'Acoustic Journeys: Exploration and the Search for an Aural History of Australia', *Australian Historical Studies*, 128, 2006, 1–17.

p. 64 'We had not been long stationary . . .', Charles Sturt, *Two Expeditions to the interior of Southern Australia, during the years 1828, 1829, 1830 and 1831* (Adelaide: Public Library of South Australia, 1963), p. 91.

p. 65 'The occasional use of fire . . .', Thomas, *Discoveries*, p. 121.

'repel rather than . . .', Hallam, 'A view from the other side', p. 141.

'they threatened the stability . . .', Hallam, 'A view from the other side', p. 151.

p. 66 'refraining from offering . . .', Hallam, 'A view from the other side', p. 151.

'These poor creatures . . .', William Dampier, *A New Voyage around the World*, vol. 1, fifth edition (London: Printed for James Knapton, 1703), p. 466.

'the natives were well pleas'd . . .', William Bradley, *A Voyage to New South Wales: The Journal of Lieutenant William Bradley RN of HMS Sirius, 1786–1792* (Sydney: The Trustees of the Public Library of New South Wales in association with Ure Smith, 1969), p. 59.

p. 67 'Without a recognition . . .', Paul Carter, *Living in a New Country: History, Travelling and Language* (London: Faber and Faber, 1992), p. 160.

p. 70 Henry Kendall, 'Sonnets on the Discovery of Botany Bay by Captain Cook', Sonnet IV, 'Sutherland's Grave', printed in *Poems of Henry Kendall* (Sydney: Angus and Robertson, 1920), p. 265.

Barron Field, 'On Visiting the Spot where Captain Cook and Sir Joseph Banks First Landed in Botany Bay', first printed in *First Fruits of Australian Poetry*, second edition (Sydney: R. Howe, 1823).

pp. 70 & 71 'In my research notes . . .' and 'seemed to insist . . .', Kim Scott, *Kayang and Me* (Fremantle: Fremantle Arts Press, 2005), p. 27 & p. 28.

p. 73 The 'Secret Instructions' from the British Admiralty to James Cook are printed in Beaglehole (ed.), *The Voyage of the Endeavour 1768–1771*, pp. cclxxix–cclxxxiv.

'first essay in anthropology', Thomas, *Discoveries*, p. 51.

p. 77 'attest to what . . .', Thomas, *Discoveries*, p. xxxiv.

p. 78 'Their eyes and hands . . .' and 'I happened to be . . .', from an extract of the voyage journal William Monkhouse printed as an appendix in Beaglehole (ed.), *The Voyage of the Endeavour 1768–1771*, p. 567.

p. 79 'displaced into the context of mimicry', Vanessa Smith, *Literary Culture and the Pacific: Nineteenth-century Textual Encounters* (Cambridge: Cambridge University Press, 1998), p. 50.

p. 80 'clear evidence the spears . . .', Clendinnen, *Dancing with Strangers*, p. 125.

p. 83 'many were the occasions . . .', Hallam, 'A view from the other side', p. 143.

'avoid encounters altogether', Hallam, 'A view from the other side', p. 143.

'sullenly hostile', G. Arnold Wood, *The Discovery of Australia* (London: Macmillan, 1922), p. 434.

p. 89 'It was well-documented . . .', Val Attenbrow, *Sydney's Aboriginal Past: Investigating the Archaeological and Historical Records* (Sydney: UNSW Press, 2003), p. 103.

'Tupaia the Indian . . .', letter from Joseph Banks to Dawson Turner FRS, cited in Anne Salmond, *The Trial of the Cannibal Dog: The Remarkable Story of Captain Cook's Encounters in the South Seas* (New Haven: Yale University Press, 2003), p. 75. The original letter can be found in the Banks Collection, MS 82, Fitzwilliam Museum, Cambridge. See Harold Carter, 'Note on the Drawings by an Unknown Artist from the Voyage of HMS *Endeavour*', in Margaret Lincoln (ed.), *Science and Exploration in the Pacific: European Voyages to the Southern Oceans in the Eighteenth Century* (Suffolk: Boydell Press in association with National Maritime Museum, 1998), pp. 133–5.

'skilled in painting . . .' and 'enthralled with . . .', Salmond, *The Trial of the Cannibal Dog*, p. 76 & p. 74.

'it was Parkinson . . .', Smith, 'The first European depictions', p. 29.

p. 90 'Europeans travelling ...', *The Salvado Memoirs: Historical Memories of Australia and Particularly of the Benedictine Mission of New Norcia and of the Habits and Customs of the Australian Natives*, translated and edited by E. J. Stormon (Nedlands, WA: UWA Press, 1977), p. 143. Rosendo Salvador's memoirs were originally published as *Memorie Storiche dell'Australia* (Rome: Society for the Propagation of the Faith, 1851).

In the end

p. 100 'the final movement ...', Hallam, 'A view from the other side', p. 150.

p. 101 'stingray in shape', Djon Mundine, 'Kamay', in *Lines in the Sand: Botany Bay Stories from 1770*, Exhibition Catalogue (Gymea: Hazelhurst Regional Gallery and Arts Centre, 2008) p. 8.

'It is not surprising ...', Thomas, *Discoveries*, p. 114.

p. 105 'an obscure event ...', Shahid Amin, *Event, Memory, Metaphor: Chauri Chaura 1922–1992* (Berkeley: University of California Press, 1995), p. 5.

'is ongoing because ...', Deborah Bird Rose, 'The Saga of Captain Cook: Remembrance and Morality', in Bain Attwood & Fiona Magowan (eds), *Telling Stories: Indigenous History and Memory in Australia and New Zealand* (Sydney: Allen & Unwin, 2001), p. 62.

p. 106 'common to Aboriginal ...', 'a means for accounting ...' and 'Cook can be considered ...', Chris Healy, 'Captain Cook: Between Black and White', in Sylvia Kleinart & Margo Neale (eds), *Oxford Companion to Art and Culture* (Melbourne: Oxford University Press, 2000), p. 92.

'mere passage of ...', Kenneth Maddock, 'Myth, history and a sense of oneself', in Jeremy Beckett (ed.), *Past and Present: The Construction of Aboriginality* (Canberra: Aboriginal Studies Press, 1988), p. 13.

'show interpretive respect ...', Chris Healy, 'We know your mob now: histories and their cultures', *Meanjin* vol. 49, no. 3 (1990) pp. 521–2.

p. 108 '... basic human encounters ...', Mark McKenna speaking on *Hindsight*, ABC Radio, 13 March 2005. For transcript of the interview, see: http://www.abc.net.au/rn/history/hindsight/stories/s1318316.htm

'official chaplain ...', P. K. Phillips, 'McEncroe, John (1794–1868)', *Australian Dictionary of Biography*, vol. 2 (Melbourne: Melbourne University Press, 1967), pp. 165–6, accessed through ADB online edition.

'apprenticed before ...', T. L. Suttor, 'Ullathorne, William Bernard (1806–1889)', *Australian Dictionary of Biography*, vol. 2 (Melbourne: Melbourne University Press, 1967) pp. 544–6, accessed through ADB online edition.

p. 109 'inside the Domain wall ...', McEncroe, *Sydney Morning Herald*, 27 April 1863. The account is also published in C. H. Bertie, 'Captain Cook and Botany Bay', *Royal Australian Historical Society Journal and Proceedings*, vol. x, part v, 1924, pp. 237–8. Unless specified in the text, all quotations from the Aboriginal man's recorded testimony are taken from the *Sydney Morning Herald*.

For the claim that the informant was Mahroot, see Keith V. Smith, 'Voices on the beach', *Lines in the Sand*, p. 13.

'it has never been . . .', *Sydney Gazette*, 16 June 1829.

'The plurality of settler sovereignty', Lisa Ford, 'Traversing the Frontiers of the History Wars: the Plurality of Settler Sovereignty in Early New South Wales', *Macquarie Law WP* 2008–1, electronic copy available at: http://ssrn.com/abstract=1090381

p. 113 'they came round . . .', 'found it necess'y . . .' and 'I gave two . . .', King's Journal, *Historical Records of New South Wales*, pp. 541–2.

'one of the females . . .', White, *Journal*, p. 118.

'this skin he seem'd much pleas'd . . .', Bradley, *A Voyage to New South Wales*, p. 99.

'of middle age . . .', Flannery (ed.), *Terra Australis*, p. 10.

p. 115 'travels were cast . . .' and 'In European history . . .', Healy, *From the Ruins*, pp. 18 & 58.

p. 116 'Thus the first gift . . .', William Ullathorne, *From Cabin-boy to Archbishop: The Autobiography of Archbishop Ullathorne* (first published in 1891) facsimile edition (London: Burns Oates, 1941), p. 67.

'By definition . . .', Healy, 'We know your mob now', p. 515.

'beginnings and endings . . .', Dening, *Islands and Beaches*, p. 32.

p. 117 'as a bearer . . .', Healy, 'We know your mob now', p. 516.

Mahroot's evidence is printed in the *Report from the Select Committee on the Condition of Aborigines*, 1845 (Fascimile copy, Canberra: Popinjay Publications, 1989).

'an impressing of . . .', Paul A. Cohen, *History in Three Keys: The Boxers as Event, Experience and Myth* (New York: Columbia University Press, 1997), p. xii.

p. 118 'following an intuition . . .' and 'plunged straight into . . .', Roland Robinson, *The Shift of Sands: An Autobiography 1952–62* (Melbourne: Macmillan, 1976), pp. 78 & 79.

'when [Captain Cook] landed . . .', 'Captain Cook', related by Percy Mumbulla, in Roland Robinson, *Altjeringa and Other Aboriginal Poems* (Sydney: A. H. & A. W. Reed, 1970), pp. 29–30. All quotes are from this version.

p. 119 'the tenacity of tradition . . .', Healy, 'We know your mob now', p. 521.

'material stuff, blankets, calico . . .', Chips Mackinolty & Paddy Wainbarrunga, 'Too many Captain Cooks', in Tony Swain and Deborah Bird Rose (eds), *Aboriginal Australians and Christian Missions* (Adelaide: Australian Association for the Study of Religions, 1981), pp. 355–60. All the quotes from the narrative are taken from this published version. Another version of the narrative was recorded on film. See: Penny MacDonald (dir.), 'Too many Captain Cooks' (Ronin Films, 1989).

- p. 121 'First there was water ...', Hobble Tanaieri, 'Foreword', in Hannah Middleton, *Now We Want the Land Back: A History of the Australian Aboriginal People* (Sydney: New Age Publishers, 1977), p. 7.

    'Virtually from my first day ...', Deborah Bird Rose, *Hidden Histories: Black Stories from Victoria River Downs, Humbert River and Wave Hill Stations* (Canberra: Aboriginal Studies Press, 1991), p. xxii.

- p. 122 'most philosophically gifted ...' and 'When [Hobbles] came around ...', Rose, *Hidden Histories*, p. xxii.

    All of the quotes from Hobbles Danaiyarri's narrative are taken from two versions that were told to and transcribed by Deborah Bird Rose. These can be found in Rose, *Hidden Histories*, pp. 15–17 and Rose, 'Remembrance', *Aboriginal History*, vol. 13, nos 1–2 (1989), pp. 138–143.

- p. 123 'a large set of people ...', Rose, *Hidden Histories*, p. xxiii.

    Billy Gibbs, in Sue Davenport, Peter Johnson and Yuwali, *Cleared Out: First Contact in the Western Desert* (Canberra: Aboriginal Studies Press, 2005), p. ii. Originally published in Sue Davenport (ed.), *Yintakaja-lampajuya: These Are Our Waterholes* (South Hedland: Western Desert Puntukurnuparna and Pilbara Aboriginal Language Centre, 1988).

    'The generally accepted view ...', Henry Reynolds, *The Law of the Land*, second edition (Ringwood: Penguin, 1992), p. 9.

- p. 124 'By relating the dispossession ...', Reynolds, *The Law of the Land*, p. 9.

- p. 125 '... met people living in the country ...', 'In Yarralin people's thinking ...' and 'I was told ...', Rose, 'The saga of Captain Cook', p. 74.

    Alan Frost, 'New South Wales as Terra Nullius: The British denial of Aboriginal land rights', *Historical Studies*, 19/77 (October 1981), pp. 513–23.

- pp. 128ff All quotes from Percy Mumbulla's narrative come from Lee Chittick and Terry Fox, *Travelling with Percy: A South Coast Journey* (Canberra: Aboriginal Studies Press, 1997), pp. 9–10.

- p. 129 'the canonical images ...', Nicholas Thomas, *Possessions: Indigenous Art, Colonial Culture* (London: Thames and Hudson, 1999) p. 200. My discussion of Gordon Bennett's painting *Possession Island* (1991) draws largely from Thomas, *Possessions*, pp. 199–208.

- p. 131 'domination and documentation', Healy, 'We know your mob now', pp. 520–21.

    The idea of 'the game of spot the difference' comes from Tina Baum's essay on Daniel Body in *Cultural Warriors: National Indigenous Art Triennial 07* (Canberra: National Gallery of Australia, 2007), p. 72.

- p. 134 'Questioning the romantic notions ...', Daniel Boyd, Artist's Statement, *Culture Warriors*, p. 71.

'felt that the portrait...', Andrew Sayers, 'In the national interest', *Portrait*, 8, Winter (2003), p. 7.

p. 135 'Jones' art is...' and 'points to something...', Odette Kelada, *Dianne Jones: Lookin Up*, Exhibition catalogue for exhibition held at Canberra Contemporary Art Space, 29 August–11 October 2008 (Canberra: Canberra Contemporary Art Space, 2008), p. 1.

'the act of piracy' and 'nationalistic rivalry', Boyd, *Culture Warriors*, p. 72.

p. 136 'With our history...', Boyd, *Culture Warriors*, p. 71.

List of Illustrations

Plate 1. Joshua Reynolds, *Sir Joseph Banks* (1771–73), oil on canvas, National Portrait Gallery, London

Plate 2. Artist unknown, Robert Molyneux (1746–1771), Master of H.M. Bark *Endeavour* (ca. 1768), Hocken Collections, Uare Taoka o Hakena, University of Otago

Plate 3. Sydney Parkinson (1745–1771), oil on board, probably a self-portrait (ca. 1770), © The Natural History Museum, London

Plate 4. Sydney Parkinson, [Two Aborigines and Canoes, 1770], © The British Library Board, All Rights Reserved, Add 9345, f. 14v

Plate 5. Thomas Chambers, *Two of the Natives of New Holland, Advancing to Combat*, Plate XXVII, in Sydney Parkinson, *A Journal of the Voyage to the South Seas, in His Majesty's Ship, The Endeavour* (London: Printed for Stanfield Parkinson, 1773)

Plate 6. J. K. Sherwin after William Hodges, *The Landing at Erramanga, one of the New Hebrides*, Plate LXII, in James Cook, *Towards the South Pole, and around the world, performed in his Majesty's ships, the Resolution and Adventure* (London: Strahan and Cadell, 1777), © The British Library Board, All Rights Reserved, Add. 23920, f. 85

Plate 7. *Captain Cook's Landing at Botany Bay AD 1770*, in *The History of Australian Discovery and Colonisation* (Sydney: Hanson and Bennett, 1865), facing page 71, National Library of Australia

Plate 8. James Basire after William Hodges, *The Landing at Mallicolo, one of the New Hebrides*, Plate LX, in James Cook, *Towards the South Pole, and around the world, performed in his Majesty's ships, the Resolution and Adventure* (London: Strahan and Cadell, 1777), National Library of Australia, nla.pic-an7691873

Plate 9. *Captain Cook's Landing at Botany, A.D. 1770*, Supplement to Town and Country Journal, 21 December 1872, National Library of Australia, nla.pic-an7890396

Plate 10. E. Phillips Fox, Australia 1865–1915, *The Landing of Captain Cook at Botany Bay 1770* (1902), oil on canvas, 192.2 × 265.4 cm, National Gallery of Victoria, Gilbee Bequest, 1902

Plate 11. John Webber [Death of Cook, ca.1781–83?], Dixson Galleries, State Library of New South Wales, Original: DG 26

Plate 12. Samuel Calvert, engraving after J. A. Gilfillan, *Captain Cook Taking Possession of the Australian Continent on Behalf of the British Crown, AD 1770, under the name of New South*

Wales, printed in Sydney Illustrated News, December 1865, National Library of Australia, nla.pic-an7682920

Plate 13. C. Richardson, Captain Cook's First Landing in Australia—'Battle of Botany Bay', in McKinley's Australian Pictorial Almanac for 1880 (Melbourne: A. McKinley, 1880), facing page 39, National Library of Australia

Plate 14. John Frederick Miller, [Five spears and a shield, 1771] © The British Library Board, All Rights Reserved, Add. 23920, f. 35

Plate 15. Spears from Botany Bay, Cook Collection © Cambridge University Museum of Archaeology and Anthropology, D1914.1–4

Plate 16. Bark shield [from Botany Bay] © The Trustees of the British Museum, All Rights Reserved, AOA Q78.Oc.839

Plate 17. John Webber, Portrait of Captain John Gore, 1780, oil on canvas, National Library of Australia, nla.pic-an2256760

Plate 18. Artist unknown, [Portrait of Surgeon William Brougham Monkhouse, ca. 1768?], pastel, National Library of Australia, nla.pic-an11554609

Plate 19. [Australian Aborigines paddling bark canoes, 1770], © The British Library Board, All Rights Reserved, Add 15508, f. 10

Plate 20. [Chart of Botany Bay, made during Captain Cook's first voyage, after April 1770], © The British Library Board, All Rights Reserved, Add. 31360, no. 33

Plate 21. [Pencil sketch of stingray by Herman Dietrich Sporing made during James Cook's first voyage 1768–1771], f. 47 in The Collection of Natural History Drawings Commissioned by Joseph Banks on the Endeavour Voyage 1768–1771, © The Natural History Museum, London

Plate 22. A Native Violet, photograph by Robyn Stacey, reproduced courtesy of the artist and Stills Gallery, Sydney.

Plate 23. Percy Mumbulla near Culburra, New South Wales (1978), photograph by Lee Chittick, reproduced courtesy of Lee Chittick, John Mumbler and AIATSIS

Plate 24. Hobbles Danaiyarri, photograph by and courtesy of Deborah Bird Rose

Plate 25. Gordon Bennett, Possession Island (1991), Historic Houses Trust, Sydney, reproduced with permission of the artist

Plate 26. Daniel Boyd, We Call Them Pirates Out Here (2006), Museum of Contemporary Art, Sydney, reproduced with permission of the artist

Plate 27. John Webber, Portrait of Captain James Cook RN (1782), National Portrait Gallery, Canberra, 2000.25

Plate 28. Dianne Jones, LHOOQ ERE! (2001), inkjet on canvas, National Gallery of Australia, Canberra, © Dianne Jones, Licensed by VISCOPY, Australia, 2008

Plate 29. Daniel Boyd, Captain No Beard (2006), oil on canvas, National Gallery of Australia, Canberra, reproduced with permission of the artist

Acknowledgments

Anyone writing today about Captain Cook has an outstandingly rich scholarship to draw upon. Much of the best of it has been produced, indeed pioneered, by Australian scholars who have been leaders at home and internationally in cross-cultural interpretations of Cook's history and memory. The enormous debt I owe to this intellectual community is, I trust, clear from my citations of their work.

The book was assisted by two research schemes. It was researched and written while I was the recipient of an Australian Research Council Post Doctoral Fellowship (DP0451114) in the School of Historical Studies at Monash University in Melbourne. Some of the research was undertaken while I was a Visiting Fellow at the National Museum of Australia in Canberra for part of 2006, and so I wish to acknowledge the generous assistance of the National Museum of Australia through its National Museum Research Fellowship Program. Final touches were added to the manuscript when I returned to the Museum in 2008 to take up a post in its newly established Centre for Historical Research.

Research for the book drew on the collections of libraries, museums, galleries and archives in Australia, New Zealand and the United Kingdom, including the National Library of Australia, the National Museum of Australia, the National Portrait Gallery and the National Gallery of Australia in Canberra; the National Gallery of Victoria in Melbourne; the Mitchell Library and Dixson Collections at the State Library of New South Wales, the Botany Bay National Park Visitor Centre, and the Museum of Contemporary Art in Sydney; the Alexander Turnbull Library in Wellington; the University of Cambridge Museum of Archaeology and Anthropology in Cambridge; and the British Library, the British Museum, the Natural History Museum and the National Archives in London. I wish to express my appreciation to staff at those institutions for answering my research inquiries, providing access to their collections, and giving permission to reproduce images. My thanks also to my research assistant Leah Bartsch, who ably assisted with picture research and copyright clearance.

At Cambridge University Press I am especially grateful to Sandra McComb for her commitment to the project, and to Frances Wade, Jodie Howell and Debbie Lee for their astute editorial advice.

Some material in the book was previously published in my article '"To try to form some connections with the natives": Encounters between Captain Cook and indigenous people at Botany Bay in 1770', *History Compass* 6/2 (2008), pp. 469–87; and in my chapter 'The encounter between Captain Cook and indigenous people at Botany Bay in 1770 reconsidered', in Peter Veth, Peter Sutton and Margo Neale (eds), *Strangers on the Shore: Early Coastal Contacts with Australia* (Canberra: National Museum of Australia, 2008), pp. 198–207.

Index

Aboriginal people
  accounts of first landing 44–6, 110–12
  body decorations 9, 10
  and canoes plates 4, 19, 44, 56–7, 88
  children 13, 40
  clans at Botany Bay 11–12
  depictions of plates 4, 5, 19, 10, 30–1, 43, 88–90
  in depictions of first landing 23, 28–9, 30–2, 37, 132–4
  at Endeavour River 64, 87–8
  fires 62, 63–5
  and first fleet 1788 10, 66–7
  fishing 6, 12–13, 42, 43, 88, 93
  and formation of a nation 36
  and gifts to 19, 52–4, 112–14
  and land rights 125
  language of 12, 18, 58
  narratives
    and Captain Cook 105–8, 111–17, 119–20, 121–3, 125–9
    and Ned Kelly 121–2
  at north head 6, 8
  at Port Jackson 12
  re-enactments 1901 28
  and shields 20–2, 40–2
  and sovereignty 109–10
  and spears 12, 22, 80, 94–5
  and spirits 55–6
  and strangers 12–13, 15–16, 60–1, 99, 102–4
    Aboriginal accounts of 110–12
    approaching 57–8, 59–60
    and burial of Sutherland 69
    communicating with 18
    defiance 8–9
    fleeing from 37–9, 55–6, 81, 82–4
    initial reactions 15
    mimicry 78–80

nonchalance of 13
observing 5–6
protecting resources 65–6
resistance 16
shouting at 62, 67–8
uninterested in 86, 87
watching from behind trees 90
in Sydney 109, 110, 117–18
in village near anchorage 13, 40, 52
weapons of 6, 8, 15, 20, 40, 57
women 13, 56
see also Gameygal people; Gurindji people; Gweagal people
Alice Springs 20
Amin, Shahid 105
Arnhem Land 119
Attenbrow, Val 89
Australia
Federation 24, 26
formation of nation 26–7, 36
history and Captain Cook 123–5
see also New Holland
Australian Pictorial Almanac, 1880 32

Balloderree 10
Banks, Joseph
and Aboriginal people 60, 65–6, 67, 76–7, 78, 87, 93, 94–5
body decorations 9
claiming canoes 56–7
communicating with 18
on first landing 15
fishing 12–13
gifts to 53, 54
on north head 5–6, 8, 9–10
shouting and smoking 62
in village 13
watching from behind trees 90
on Bare Island 67–8
on countryside 94
and Dampier's journal 8–9
decision to sail westward from NZ 4
in depictions of first landing 23–4, 33, 34, 133–4
on discovering Botany Bay 3
end of first day 47
exploration of countryside 52, 73–4
journals 40, 91

INDEX

 landings on way north 72
 plant collecting 55, 65, 82, 87, 91, 93, 99, 101
 portraits *plate 1*, 25
 preparing for landing 14–15
 re-enactments 1901 27, 28
 and shields 21–2, 40
 on spears 42, 43
 specimen collecting 90
 on Tupaia 89
 on use of weapons 21, 22
Banksmeadow 94
Bare Island 67
Basire, James, *The Landing at Mallicolo, one of the New Hebrides* *plate 8*, 29
Bass, George 15–16
Bateman Bay 17
Baudin, Nicholas 60, 63
Beaglehole, John Cawte 54
Bediagal people 11
Bennett, Gordon 129, 130–1
 Possession Island *plate 25*, 130, 131
Bluitt 45
Bootie, John 76
Botany Bay
 charts 11, *plate 20*
 discovered 3
 Endeavour leaves 138
 Endeavour sails into 10–11
 naming of 101
 sounding of 5, 6
 see also landing at Botany Bay; possession ceremony
Bowdler, Sandra 53
Boyd, Daniel
 Captain No Beard *plate 29*, 135
 King No Beard 135
 We Call Them Pirates Out Here *plate 26*, 131–6
Bradley, William 113
Brewster, Anne 31–2
Briscoe, Peter 14
British Library, London 19, 89
British Museum 40
Brush Island 17
Buchan, Alexander 10
Buchan, Bruce 53
Bulli 17
Bullmayne 45

Bumbera Point 46
burial of Sutherland 69–71
Bustard Bay 72
Byrne, Denis 53
Byron, John 75

Calvert, Samuel, *Captain Cook Taking Possession of the Australian Continent, on Behalf of the British Crown, AD 1770* plate 12
Cambridge Museum of Archaeology and Anthropology 42, 43
Cambridge University 42
canoes *plates* 4, 19, 44, 56–7, 88
Cape Farewell, New Zealand 3–4
Captain Cook's Landing at Botany Bay AD 1770 (published 1865) *plate* 7
Captain Cook's Landing at Botany Bay, A.D. 1770 (published 1872) *plate* 9
carpenters 52
Carter, Paul 63, 67
Chambers, Thomas, *Two of the Natives of New Holland, Advancing to Combat* plate 5, 30–1
children, Aboriginal 13, 40
Chittick, Lee 118
Cipriani, G. B. 29
Clark, Manning 75
Clendinnen, Inga 16, 80–1
Collins, David 11
Collins, Diane 63
communication
  language 6–7, 12, 18, 58
  shouting 62–3, 67–8
  using signs 6, 18, 19
Cook, Elizabeth 15
Cook, James
  in Aboriginal narratives 105–8, 114–17, 118–20, 121–7, 127–9
  and Aboriginal people 54, 77, 85–7, 90–1, 94, 100, 102
    approaching 60, 67
    communicating with 18
    at Endeavour River 87–8
    at first landing 13–14, 16
    gifts to 19, 52, 71, 112
    instructions for voyage 73
    retreating 37–9, 55, 81, 82–3
    village 40
  and Australian history 26–7, 122–5
  and Botany Bay 3, 13–15, 51, 65, 137
    charts of 11, *plate* 20
  at Brush Island 17

and canoes 44
as Captain 35
on countryside 86
death 128–9
    depictions of *plate 11*
in depictions of first landing 23–4, 29, 30, 32–4, 132–3
exploration of country 52, 73–5
and fires 64
and first landing 16–18, 33–4
journals 19, 29, 31, 44–5, 91
landings on way north 72
in New Zealand 39–40
portraits *plates* 27, 28, 29, 25, 134–6
possession ceremony 35
re-enactments 1901 26, 27–8
and shields 22
use of weapons 19–21
voyage from New Zealand 3–4
Cox, Matthew 52
cross-culture encounters
    dealing with strangers 12–13
    and language 6–7, 18
    mimicry 79–80
    noises of 62–3
    see also Aboriginal people and strangers; gifts to Aboriginal people

Daguragu 120–1
Dampier, William 8–9, 66
Danaiyarri, Hobbles *plate* 24, 121–7
    see also Tanaieri, Hobble
Dark, Eleanor 56
Dening, Greg 4, 20, 116
Dharawal language 12
Dolmoik 45
Dolphin 5, 75
Douglass, Henry Grattan 110
Dozey, John 52
Duchamp Marcel 135

Earle, Augustus 117
Edgecombe, John 65
Endeavour
    at Botany Bay 4–5, 10–11, 17
        anchors near south shore 12, 13
        leaves 137

    wind delays departure 92, 99
  cleaning of 82
  damage to 72
  in depictions of first landing 23, 31
  details of 51
  at Endeavour River 64, 72
  logs of voyage 21
  replenished 92
  sailing up east coast 72
  ship's company 52, 76
  voyage from New Zealand 3–4
Endeavour Bay 42
Endeavour River 44, 58–9, 72
  Aboriginal people at 64, 87–8
Erskine, Nigel 5

Field, Barron 70
fires 62, 63–5
first fleet and Aboriginal people 10, 66–7
fishing 6, 12–13, 42, 43, 88, 93
  by mariners 61, 75, 76, 100
flags, in depictions of first landing 34, 36–7
Flinders, Matthew 9, 12, 15–16, 20, 79, 113
Ford, Lisa 109
Forwood, Stephen 103
Fox, Emanuel Phillips, *The Landing of Captain Cook at Botany Bay 1770* plate 10, 23–5, 131
  composition of 31–2, 127
  depictions of Aboriginal people 23, 28, 31–2, 37
  depictions of Cook 23–4, 32–4
  flags 34, 36–7
  possession ceremony 36–7
  reproductions of 136
  research for painting 25–6
Frost, Alan 125

Gameygal people 11
George III, King 135
Georges River 11
Gibbs, Billy 123
gifts to Aboriginal people 19, 52–4, 59, 71, 111–14, 117–19, 120
Gilfillan, John Alexander, *Captain Cook Taking Possession of the Australian Continent on Behalf of the British Crown in 1770* 34, 35, 129, 130
Gore, John plate 17, 75–7
Gurindji people 120–2

INDEX

Gweagal people 11, 73

Haite, Francis 52
Hallam, Sylvia 9–10, 12–13, 57–8, 60, 82, 100
Hawkesworth, John 29, 31, 44–5
haycutting 65–6
Healy, Chris 27, 37, 106, 115, 116, 131
Hicks, Zachary 57, 58, 59–60, 72, 112
History of Australian Discovery and Colonisation, 1865 44–6
Hocken Library, New Zealand 5
Hodges, William 29
Howard, Janette 134
Howard, John 134
Howitt, A. W. 7–8
Hughes, Richard 52

Indigenous people
   see Aboriginal people; Maori

Jervis Bay 17
Johnson, Isaac 52
Jones, Dianne, LHOOQ 'ERE! *plate* 28, 135
Jones, Thomas 52
Jordon, Benjamin 52
journals
   Dampier's 8–9
   of voyage 19, 29, 30, 31, 40, 44–5, 76, 78, 91
   writing of 6–7

Kelada, Odette 135
Kelly, Ned 121
Kendall, Henry, 'Sutherland's Grave' 69–70
King Georges Sound 79
King, Philip Gidley 112–13
Kooriwal 46
Kurrul 45

La Pérouse, Jean-François de Galaup 46
land rights 123, 124–5
landing at Botany Bay
   Aboriginal accounts of 44–6, 110–12
   commemorative plaque 110
   depictions of *plates* 7, 9, 10, 13, 26, 23–4, 28–9, 30–4, 36–7, 131–4, 135–6
   and formation of a nation 26–7
   on north shore 44

preparing for 14–15
   re-enactments 1901 26, 27–8
   re-enactments 1970 120–1
   use of shields 21–2
   use of weapons 19–21
   see also possession ceremony
landing party 13, 14–15, 40
   in depictions of first landing 23–4, 29, 30, 32
   on north shore 44
   re-enactments 1901 28
language
   of Aboriginal people 12, 18, 58
   and cross-culture encounters 6–7, 18
   shouting 62–3, 67–8
Littleboy, Michael 52
local people
   see Aboriginal people; Maori

McEncroe, John 108, 109, 110–12
McKenna, Mark 108
Macquarie River 63–4
Maddock, Kenneth 106
Mahroot 109, 117
Manly 80–1
Maori 18, 78
mariners
   and Aboriginal people 57–8, 59, 61, 65–6, 77, 93, 99–100
   burial of 69–71
   collection of water and wood 51–2
   and first landing 14–15
   fishing 61, 75, 76, 100
   journals 6–7
   see also landing party
Middleton, Hannah 120–1
Miller, John Frederick, drawings of plate 14, 41, 43
Moey, Samuel 52
Molyneux, Robert plate 2, 5, 6, 76
Monkhouse, Jonathon 76
Monkhouse, William Brougham plate 18, 78, 85, 86, 94–5
Morton, Earl of 16, 18
Mulvaney, John 61
Mumbulla, King Jacky 119
Mumbulla, Percy plate 23, 118–19, 127–9
Mundine, Djon 101

National Gallery of Victoria 24
National History Museum, London 10
National Library of Australia, Canberra 76, 78
National Portrait Gallery of Australia 135
Ned Kelly in Aboriginal narratives 121
New Holland 4, 17, 59
    exploration of country 52, 72, 73–5, 85, 86, 94
    landings on 16–18, 72
    see also Botany Bay; possession ceremony
New Zealand 3–4, 18, 20, 39–40, 71, 78
Novell, George 52

oysters 75, 76

paintings, historical accuracy of 24, 25–6
Pariera, Manoel 52
Parkins, Ray 51, 52
Parkinson, Sydney *plate* 3, 10, 18, 22, 30, 89–90, 101
    drawings of *plate* 4, 10, 30, 41, 43, 44, 90
Peckover, William 52
Phillip, Captain Arthur 15, 63, 86, 112–13
Phillip, Governor 80–1
Philosophical Society of Australasia 110
Pickersgill, Richard 101, 102–3
pinnace 5, 6, 14
plant collecting 55, 65, 82, 87, 91, 93, 99, 101–2
Point Hicks 17, 59
Pollock, Jackson, *Blue Poles Number 11* (1952) 130–1
Ponto, Antonio 52
Port Jackson 12, 138
'Port Jackson Painter' 10
possession ceremony 35–6
    depictions of *plates* 12, 25, 34, 36–7, 130, 131
Possession Island 35
Potta 45
Poverty Bay, New Zealand 18, 78

Quiros 4

re-enactments of first landing
    1901 26, 27–8, 35–6
    1970 120–1
Reynolds, Henry 123, 124
Reynolds, Joshua, *Sir Joseph Banks* plate 1

Richardson, C., *Captain Cook's First Landing in Australia - 'Battle of Botany Bay'* plate 13
Robertson, George 75–6
Robinson, Roland 118
Rose, Deborah Bird 105, 121–2, 125–6, 127
Royal Society 20
Royal Society, Melbourne 34

Salvado, Bishop 90
Sandwich, Earl of 42
Satterly, John 52
Saunders, Patrick 76
Sayers, Andrew 134
Scott, Kim 70–1
scymeters 6, 8
Select Committee on the Aborigines 117
shells 55, 67–8
Sherwin, J. K., *The Landing at Erramanga, one of the New Hebrides* plate 6, 29
shields plates 14, 16, 21–2, 40–2
shouting 62–3, 67–8
signs (as communication) 6, 18, 19
Simpson, Alexander 52
Smith, Bernard 10, 29, 30, 89–90
Smith, Isaac 15
Smith, Keith Vincent 109
Solander, Daniel 27
    and Aboriginal people 81
    in depictions of first landing 23, 34
    exploration of country 52, 72, 73, 85, 86
    and first landing 14–15, 21
    plant collecting 55, 65, 82, 99, 101
    portraits 25
    re-enactments 1901 27–8, 37
sounding Botany Bay 5, 6
sovereignty and Aboriginal people 109–10
spears plates 14, 15, 20, 22, 42–4, 57, 80, 94–5
Spencer, Baldwin 20
Sporing, Herman Dietrich 100–1
    sketch of stingray plate 21
Sting Ray Harbour 101
stingrays plate 21, 100–1
Sturt, Charles 63–4
Supreme Court of New South Wales 109
Sutherland, Forby 68–71
'Sutherland's Grave' 69–70

Tahiti 71, 75–6
Tanaieri, Hobble 120–2
  see also Danaiyarri, Hobbles
Terra nullius 124–5
Terrel, Edward 52
Thirsty Sound 72
Thomas, Nicholas 19, 20, 32, 44, 54, 65, 73, 77, 101–2, 130, 131
throwing sticks 57
Trinity College, Cambridge 42–3
Tungeei 119
Tunley, James 52
Tupaia
  and Aboriginal people 18–19, 64, 81
  depictions of 34, 131
  drawings of plate 19, 88–90
  and first landing 14–15
  in New Zealand 18
  and Parkinson 89–90
  and parrots 82
Turbet, Peter 12
Tuross River 118
turtles 64
Two of the Natives of New Holland, Advancing to Combat (by T. Chambers) plate 5, 30–1

Ullathorne, William 108–9, 110–11, 116

village at Botany Bay 13, 40, 52

Wainburrunga, Paddy Fordham 119
Wallis, Captain Samuel 5, 75
water collection 51–2
weapons
  Aboriginal 6, 8, 15, 20, 40, 57
  Cook's use of 19–21
  and mariners 14–15
  see also spears
Webber, John
  The Death of Cook plate 11, 32
  Portrait of Captain James Cook plate 27, 135
  Portrait of Captain John Gore plate 17
West, Obed 45
White, John 10, 113
Whitlam, Gough 130
Wilkinson 82
Willey, Keith 55–6

Williams, Glyndwr 54
women, Aboriginal 13, 56
wood collection 51–2
Wood, George Arnold 75, 83–4
Wren Library, Cambridge 42–3

Yadyer 45
Yarralin 121–2, 125

PLATE 1

Portrait by Joshua Reynolds of Joseph Banks (1743–1820), gentleman on the *Endeavour*

PLATE 2
Robert Molyneux (1746–1771), master on the *Endeavour*

PLATE 3
Sydney Parkinson (1745–1771), artist on the *Endeavour*

PLATE 4
Sydney Parkinson's page of drawings made at Botany Bay in 1770

PLATE 5
Thomas Chambers' etching *Two of the Natives of New Holland, Advancing to Combat* (published 1773)

PLATE 6
The Landing at Erramanga, one of the New Hebrides (published 1777)

PLATE 7
Captain Cook's Landing at Botany Bay AD 1770 (published 1865)

◦ PLATE 8 ◦
The Landing at Mallicolo, one of the New Hebrides (published 1777)

◦ PLATE 9 ◦
Captain Cook's Landing at Botany, A.D. 1770 (published 1872)

PLATE 10

The Landing of Captain Cook at Botany Bay 1770, E. Phillips Fox (1902)

⌒ PLATE 11 ⌒

The Death of Cook by John Webber (c. 1781–83)

⌒ PLATE 12 ⌒

Captain Cook Taking Possession of the Australian Continent, on Behalf of the British Crown, AD 1770, engraving after John Alexander Gilfillan by Samuel Calvert (published 1865)

PLATE 13
Captain Cook's First Landing in Australia—'Battle of Botany Bay' (published 1880)

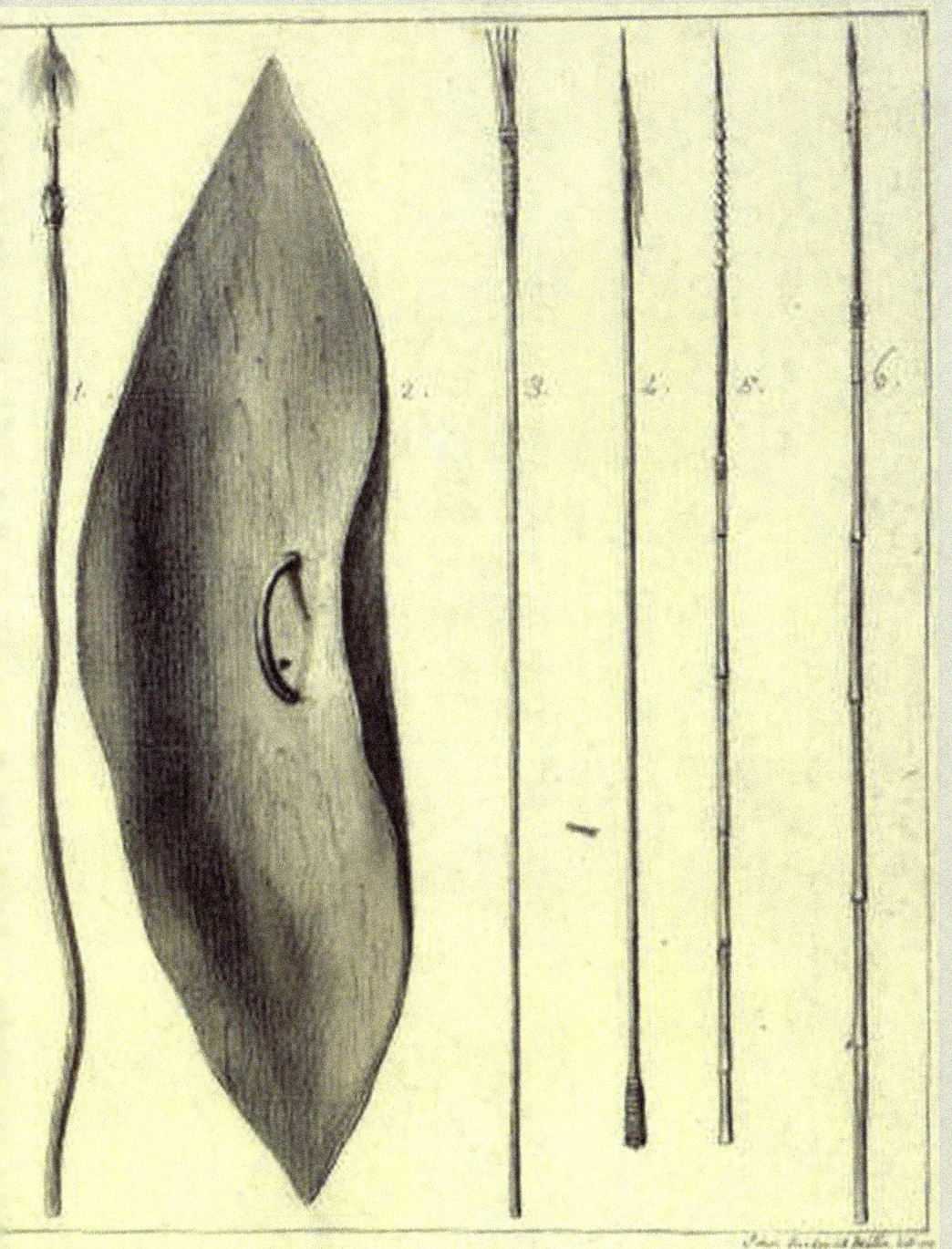

PLATE 14
John Frederick Miller's drawings of a shield and spears (1771)

PLATE 15
Spears collected at Botany Bay in 1770

PLATE 16
Bark shield collected at Botany Bay in 1770

PLATE 17
John Gore (1729?–1790), third lieutenant on the *Endeavour*

PLATE 18

William Brougham Monkhouse (?–1770), surgeon on the Endeavour

PLATE 19
Tupaia's drawing made at Botany Bay in 1770

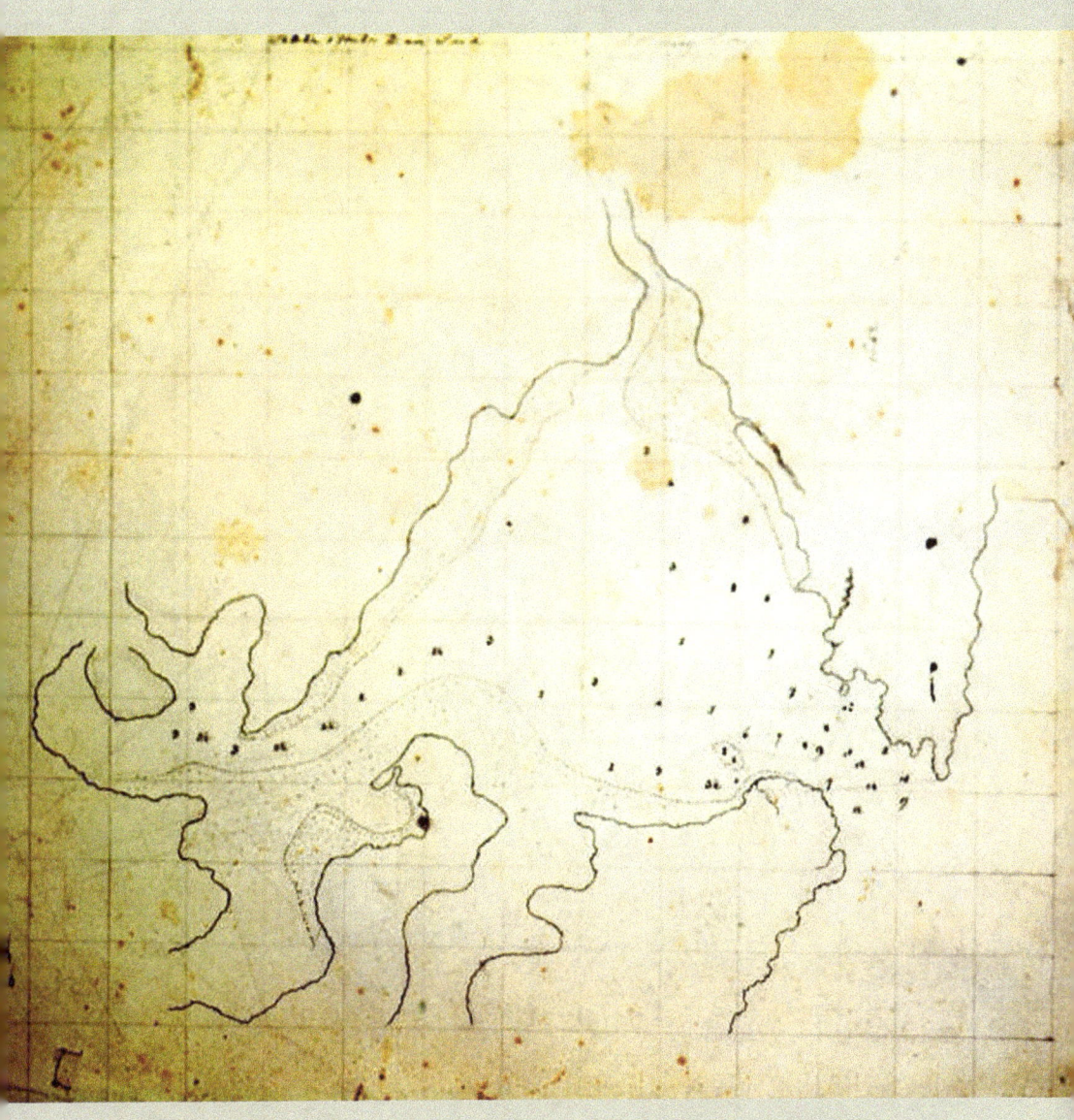

PLATE 20
Cook's chart of Botany Bay, c. 1770.

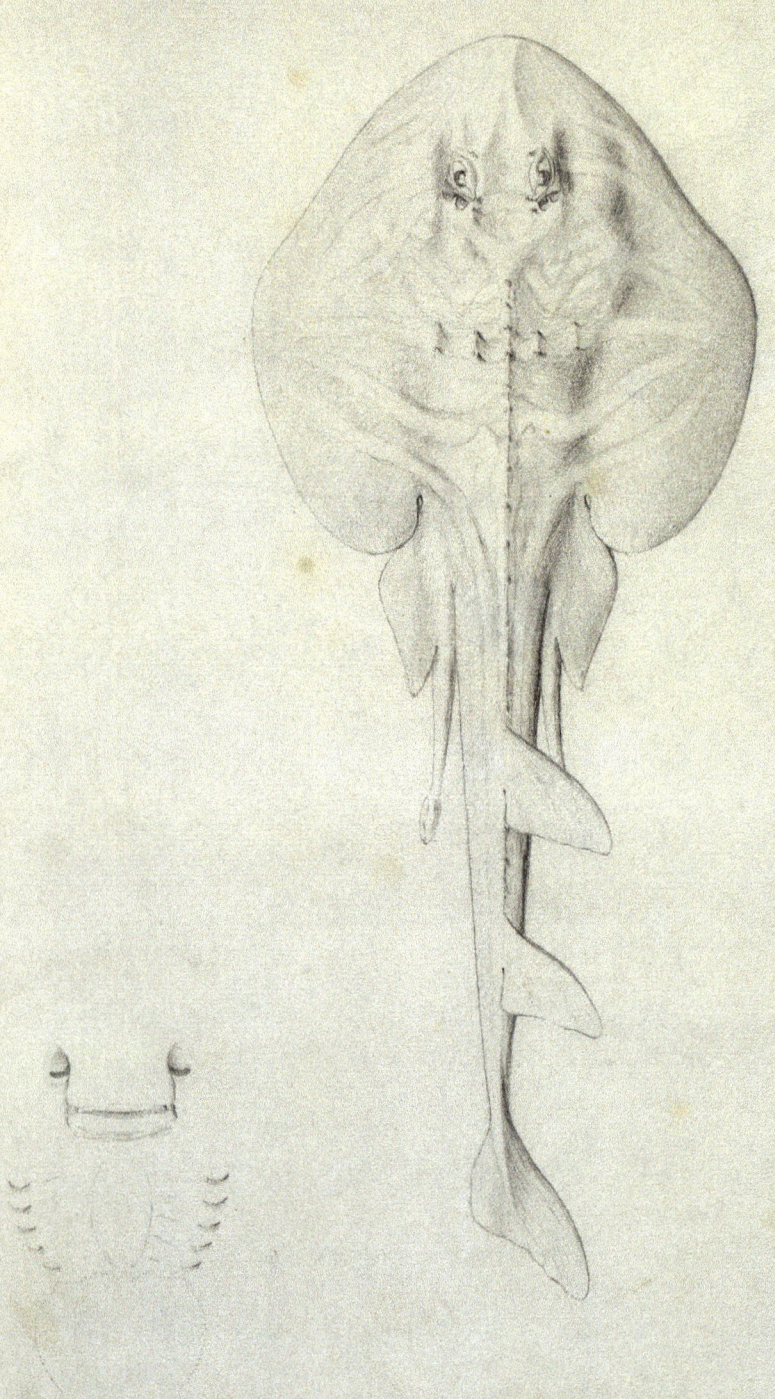

PLATE 21
Herman Sporing's drawing of a stingray caught at Botany Bay in 1770

PLATE 22
A native violet collected by Joseph Banks at Botany Bay in 1770

⸺ Plate 23 ⸺
Percy Mumbulla (c.1905–1991)

⸺ Plate 24 ⸺
Hobbles Danaiyarri (c.1925–1988)

PLATE 25
Possession Island (1991), Gordon Bennett

PLATE 26
We Call Them Pirates Out Here (2006), Daniel Boyd

PLATE 27
Portrait of Captain James Cook (1782), John Webber

PLATE 28

LHOOQ 'ERE! (2001), Dianne Jones

PLATE 29
Captain No Beard (2006), Daniel Boyd

For EU product safety concerns, contact us at Calle de José Abascal, 56–1°, 28003 Madrid, Spain or eugpsr@cambridge.org.